MASTERING the SILENCE

Strategies

for winning

the battles

of the mind

DOUG JONES

MASTERING *the* SILENCE

By Doug Jones

FAITH LIBRARY PUBLICATIONS®

23 22 21 20 19 18 17   12 11 10 09 08 07 06

Mastering the Silence
ISBN-13: 978-0-89276-970-4
ISBN-10: 0-89276-970-X

In the U.S. write:
Kenneth Hagin Ministries
P.O. Box 50126
Tulsa, OK 74150-0126
1-888-28-FAITH
rhema.org

In Canada write:
Kenneth Hagin Ministries of Canada
P.O. Box 335, Station D
Etobicoke (Toronto), Ontario
Canada M9A 4X3
1-866-70-RHEMA
rhemacanada.org

CONTENTS

From My Heart

Ministering now since 1975, I have been asked by some why I have moved into the arena of writing books. For me it is obvious; let me explain. Within the Body of Christ there are preachers and then there are teachers. The preacher declares; the preacher proclaims to the people the goodness of God. His message is focused more upon what God has done for man than on the responsibilities of man toward God. The preacher declares boldly what God has done for man through His great plan of redemption and love. More than ever, this world of ours could benefit immensely from true gospel preachers.

Teachers, on the other hand, lay necessary foundations and understanding, enabling each of us to become a productive member within the Body of Christ. The function of the teacher is that of an explainer, simplifying our responsibilities first toward God, second toward ourselves, and third toward others.

My desire as a Bible teacher has been to discover and promote the core issues of Christianity—to unveil the foundational issues that will ultimately make living the Christian life obtainable by all who profess themselves to be children of our soon-coming King. For me, the printed page is the purest vehicle through which to pass on what I have gleaned from God's Holy Word. It allows me the opportunity to address the entirety of a subject, not just the highlights. And more importantly, it allows the reader to ponder closely during devotional times the thoughts that are contained within each page.

In my search to discover the foundational issues of our faith, it became apparent that the maintenance of one's mind was a must. However, as I endeavored to simplify the whys and hows of this subject, it became clear that this was a much bigger issue than I ever imagined.

Therefore, this entire work is dedicated to the subject of the maintenance of our minds—why we must and how we are to bridle our thought life. For too long I have witnessed dear saints who have failed to control what they allow their minds to embrace. Ignorance of our individual responsibilities concerning this all-important subject has increased to unacceptable proportions within the Body of Christ.

All levels of today's society are feeling the effects of the unbridled mind. Whether we are observing the ultrarich or the impoverished, failure to maintain one's thought life has cost many their marriage. It has led teenagers into a life of rebellion against their parents and civil authorities. It has led once stable, productive individuals into a life of depression, hopelessness, and despair. The unmaintained mind has escorted many into sexual relationships that are outside of the marriage covenant. Those addicted to pornography, drugs, and alcohol are proof of the need to understand our responsibility to bridle our thoughts. Those who lie, cheat, and refuse to forgive their fellow man are revealing their ignorance concerning this core issue or have failed to apply what they know concerning the proper maintenance of their thought life.

Sounds bad. It *is* bad! The unmaintained mind is the mother of humanity's entire moral decline.

You might be reading this and thinking, *Well, I really do not fit into any of those previously mentioned categories.* Good for you! But do you have trouble working as unto the Lord on your job because thoughts of not being appreciated bombard you? Are you being affected by thoughts that you will never escape the hold that sickness has on you? Are you being influenced by thoughts of being trapped because you're a stay-at-home mom and all of your friends are pursuing their careers? Are you slowly drifting away from the belief that God really cares about you?

No, my dear friend, all of us have within us areas where we have failed to maintain our thought life, whether we like to admit it or not. Therefore, to you I dedicate this book. I believe that there is a simple solution to this problem, and it is found within the Word of God. Prayerfully consider the following chapters, for within them you will find the ingredients necessary to put you in control of your thoughts as God intended from the beginning.

The Battle and Our Armour

The battle within the mind is unavoidable. It has been and will continue to be fought by every person regardless of nation, tribe, and tongue until Jesus returns in all of His glory. This conflict knows no age limits; no one is immune from experiencing it.

Early within our life, this battle within our mind becomes evident. Many of us can remember being given permission to reach into the cookie jar for our favorite cookie. But just before we do, our mom limits our joy with the all-too-familiar words, "Just two." In spite of her imposed limitations, we can taste those goodies well before our little hands have seized even one. As we carefully lift the lid, suddenly a battle begins to rage, and from out of nowhere a thought of sneaking a third cookie eases into the realm of possibility. *"Mommy will never know. Bruce did it yesterday. Go ahead; it will be okay!"*

All of us can finish this flashback in time with our own unique memories. We might have been only four or five years of age when we first encountered this dilemma. But for me, this is one of my first recollections of experiencing a battle within my mind.

As we think back for a moment, a multitude of memories begins to surface from within the archives of our mind. Many of us can remember sitting in Third Grade taking a test. Suddenly, the thought races through our little mind, *"You didn't study for this exam, did you?"* Without a moment's hesitation, you know the answer. And in a flash, a second thought comes: *"But Straight-A Mary's paper is well within view. Just copy off of hers. Now keep your head down. If you try hard enough, you'll be able to read off of her paper . . . ."*

As our memories carry us into our teenage years, once again we are reminded that, yes, it is true: we have been fighting this battle within our mind for a very long time.

As a thirteen-year-old growing up in Michigan, I remember well initiating a game of hide-'n'-go-seek with the boys who lived at the end of the street. These boys were a little younger than I was, and I normally did not play with them. But that day I had a mission in mind. You see, their dad was the Lay's potato chip distributor for our area and, more importantly, he stored those precious potato chips in his garage.

Now Lay's potato chips are my favorite—even to this day. To borrow a phrase from a well-known television series, "the mission, if I chose to accept it," was to distract these little non-friend neighbor kids long enough for me to gain access to the garage and eat "just one." But as you know, you can't eat just one Lay's potato chip.

Successfully initiating the hide-'n'-go-seek game, I designated the garage as home base. With my plan finally in motion, I suggested that I be the first to count to a hundred and that they go hide, waiting for me to find them. Off they went to hide, and I began to count. But what these little ones did not know is that I can count out loud and eat my favorite chips at the same time. What a memory!

Sneaking extra cookies, cheating on a test, and eating chips in a garage may all be fun things to remember. But more important is the lesson revealed through these experiences, and that is, they would never have occurred had it not been for thoughts. Each of these experiences was allowed entrance into my life as the result of failing to maintain my thought life properly.

As in any battle, there are consequences in losing. The consequences of losing this battle within our mind as a five-year-old may only be getting our hands slapped and the third cookie taken away. (Oh, the misery of failing to maintain our thought life!)

Failing to maintain our thought life produces consequences, and consequences seem to increase in severity with age. I was one of those third graders who cheated on a test. The moment I was caught, the teacher immediately gave me a failing grade. Furthermore, I was invited to spend a little time in the principal's office, and before I knew it, I had a note pinned to my coat for my mother to read. Then, to make matters worse, I learned that I was not to know the full price for failing to properly maintain my thought life until "your father gets home."

As a teenager, I found that the price for failing to maintain my thought life was much greater than the intense lecture I received from my father for cheating on the test. How well I remember that horrible day when I returned from school and the can of Lay's potato chips I had helped myself to a week earlier was now sitting in the living room waiting for "your father to get home." I soon discovered that my parents were not as fond of Lay's potato chips as I was. After what seemed like the longest lecture on record, I found myself going from door to door looking for yards to mow so that I could earn money to repay my parents for the cost of the can of chips. Looking back, I see clearly that all of the negative consequences I experienced could have been avoided had I learned early on the importance of maintaining my thought life.

As we mature in life, the price for failing to maintain our thought life increases in severity.

I must admit that all of this reminiscing has caused that warm fuzzy feeling to well up within me. But hidden among all of these memories is a truth that we must consider: As we mature in life, the price for failing to maintain our thought life increases in severity.

The sufferings of a five-year-old are insignificant compared with the consequences that an adult experiences when they have failed to maintain their thought life properly. With this in mind, I encourage you to stop for a moment and consider the lives of those around you. You will soon become conscious of torn and tattered lives—lives that have been affected by humanity's failure to bridle what they allow themselves to think on.

As you look into the lives of those around you, you will observe some who have been torn by hatred—hatred directed toward civil authorities, their employers, fellow employees, or friends. For others, hatred dominates their behavior toward their parents, their spouse, and even toward their own children. As you observe these dear ones, it becomes evident that hatred allowed into our life is a destructive thing. No good thing can come from it. Hatred destroys relationships and will eventually separate us from others. It is so sad to watch someone who has been dominated by hatred grow old alone. Isolation from others has never been God's will for our life.

We must understand that such hatred begins silently within the mind and is incubated over time. As we mentally rehearse what was said or done, we allow the offense to grow to such proportions within us that it soon begins to affect our attitude toward the other

individual. And before we know it, this hatred begins to
influence our actions and words to the degree that it
slowly but steadily deteriorates the relationship. All of
this is the sad result of our failure to maintain our
thought life as we should.

As we continue to consider the lives of those around
us, we will observe marriages that have become weakened by jealousy and anger. The joy and companionship
of the marriage relationship have been eroded over time
because husbands and wives have chosen not to maintain their thought life properly. For whether we want to
admit it or not, the deterioration of a marriage begins
with our failure to scrutinize the thoughts we allow ourselves to embrace about our spouse.

*Thought always
precedes action.*

Divorce has become a way of life
in today's society, with adultery
being one of the primary causes. It is
obvious that the sufferings of divorce
when adultery is present could have been avoided if the
person who committed the adulterous act would simply
have maintained their thought life properly. There is no
adultery without thinking about it first. Thought always
precedes action. It is so sad, but in today's society,
divorce has become the monument that memorializes
the result of losing this war within the mind.

Some have cited unbridled anger, an out-of-control
temper, or selfishness as the reason for the divorce. But
long before the anger, temper, or selfishness was

manifested, we can be sure that there were little thoughts about their spouse that were allowed to remain and grow until finally things exploded emotionally.

When divorce occurs, for whatever reason, it simply reveals that someone within the marriage relationship allowed themselves to embrace thoughts that should have been rejected long ago. Thoughts—little thoughts—will eventually produce destructive and damaging conduct if given enough time and when nurtured properly. Our divorce courts can attest to this daily.

Oh, the suffering that has come upon mankind because we have chosen not to maintain our thought life properly! This failure has opened the door for our lives to be controlled and dominated by rebellion, worry, depression, envy, fornication, lying, unforgiveness, fear, and such like. When a man's sexual appetite is fueled by pornography, we suddenly realize the tremendous price that one pays for failing to maintain one's thought life. Ultimately, the price for failing to maintain our thoughts is a quality of life that dips far below what our loving Heavenly Father intends for us, His children.

Good News

But I have good news for you, dear reader. God understands our plight. He understands that we humans in and of ourselves lack sufficient abilities and means to adequately bridle our thought life. Therefore, our Heavenly Father has made available equipment—or as He calls it, "armour"—that we may use in order to win this battle within the mind.

So where do we begin? The Bible teaches plainly that we are being destroyed for the lack of knowledge (Hosea 4:6). Therefore, our only hope is to come to know the truth about this war within our mind and the armour with which we are to clothe ourselves. Without this knowledge, the casualties will continue to increase and humanity's quality of life will continue to diminish.

It seems that the corridor that will lead us toward victory begins with an understanding of this "whole armour" that we are encouraged by God to put on. This armour is described clearly by Paul in his letter to the Ephesians.

EPHESIANS 6:10-17

10 **Finally, my brethren, be strong in the Lord, and in the power of his might.**

11 **Put on the whole armour of God, that ye may be able to stand against the wiles of the devil.**

12 **For we wrestle not against flesh and blood, but against principalities, against powers, against the rulers of the darkness of this world, against spiritual wickedness in high places.**

13 **Wherefore take unto you the whole armour of God, that ye may be able to withstand in the evil day, and having done all, to stand.**

14 Stand therefore, having your loins girt about with truth, and having on the breastplate of righteousness;

15 And your feet shod with the preparation of the gospel of peace;

16 Above all, taking the shield of faith, wherewith ye shall be able to quench all the fiery darts of the wicked.

17 And take the helmet of salvation, and the sword of the Spirit, which is the word of God.

The intensity of Paul's admonishment, along with his chosen symbolism of a Roman soldier's armour, suggests strongly that if we choose not to comply—if we choose not to put on the whole armour—defeat is inevitable.

However, more important than Paul's description of each piece of armour is an instruction which he gives twice. Notice closely his words, found in verses 11 and 13: *"Put on the whole armour of God . . ."* and *"Wherefore take unto you the whole armour of God . . . ."*

Success Does Not Depend on One Piece of Armour Alone

The word "whole" is the key, for it reveals that no one piece of this armour can ensure Christian success. Apparently, every piece is to be present and working properly within us in order for us to remain on the victory side in the midst of this conflict.

Consequently, we must not allow ourselves to focus entirely on our favorite piece of armour. For example, many have specialized only in faith, thinking that it and it alone will ensure success. Others have convinced themselves that putting on righteousness is all they need in order to be victorious. How far from the truth they are! This mindset will ultimately have devastating consequences. No single piece of armour can produce complete victory in our life. We must put on the *whole* armour of God.

Misdirected Attention

As we read Paul's admonishment to put on the whole armour of God, I find it interesting that many have allowed their attention to become entirely focused upon each individual piece of the Roman soldier's armour. Consequently, many have spent countless hours researching the various pieces that made up the armour of the Roman soldier.

I fell into this trap myself, spending endless hours attempting to discover what the shield of a Roman soldier was made of. Oh, how I longed to know how long, wide, and thick it was, and exactly how it was used in war. And of course there was the sword. Wow! Its sharpness and strength caused great excitement within me as I visualized the damage it could inflict on my enemy.

I assumed that at the end of my research I would be able to insert all of this newfound knowledge about the armour of a Roman soldier back into the passage and suddenly understand clearly what Paul was telling me to do. But for me personally, knowing how long, wide, and thick a shield was brought me no closer to understanding how I was *to use* the shield of faith. I was no more enlightened than before I began my quest. Something was wrong.

Still lacking clarity as to how I was to use this armour, I concluded that just maybe the answer lay within an understanding of the relationship that each piece of armour shared with the other pieces. My quest led me to conclude that because the loins were to be girt about with truth, then truth was to act like the belt of a soldier's armour. And this belt probably held up the breastplate, further suggesting that the sword would be found suspended from the belt when not in use.

Once again, I revisited the Ephesians passage. I inserted my findings, but to my sadness, I found myself no closer to a workable understanding of how this armour was to function in my life.

Fueled by frustration but knowing that I *must* understand Paul's admonishment to put on the whole armour of God, I revisited the Roman soldier. As I visualized a soldier in full armour, I mistakenly concluded that the helmet protects the head; therefore, the helmet of salvation protects our mind. Then I wondered if the breastplate protects the soldier's vital organs, such as the heart and lungs. If that be true, then maybe the breastplate of righteousness protects the heart of the believer. Could it be possible that I had found the answer to my need for clarity? Could it be possible that, just as each piece of natural armour protects its corresponding body part, so also each piece of "the whole armour of God" protects a corresponding part of our inner man?

I immediately returned to the passage in Ephesians chapter 6 and began to insert my findings. And I was satisfied with my conclusions until I got to the "loins girt about with truth" issue. Then the question arose, What did the belt protect? And then my attention drifted to the "feet shod," and once again I found myself stumped.

Clarity seemed to be eluding me. I was baffled as to the logic behind Paul's use of a Roman soldier's armour to teach me about this spiritual armour that I must put on. What was he endeavoring to teach me? Sadly, all the knowledge I had gained about a soldier's armour failed to provide clarity and a practical way for me to comply with Paul's instructions.

A Little Closer to the Truth

As I continued my search for clarity, these questions begged to be asked. Could it be that I had been misled into placing an unwarranted amount of importance on the individual pieces that make up a Roman soldier's armour while missing the main issue that Paul was endeavoring to express? Could it be that the only reason Paul referred to a Roman soldier and his armour was to stress to us the severity of this battle? Was he saying that if I choose not to put on the "whole armour of God," I will experience defeat as quickly as a soldier in the midst of a battle would if he failed to put on his protective armour?

My suspicions were validated when I discovered a passage in First Thessalonians. The Apostle Paul, writing this time to the church at Thessalonica, says, *"But let us, who are of the day, be sober, putting on the breastplate of faith and love; and for an helmet, the hope of salvation"* (1 Thess. 5:8).

As I compared what Paul said to the Thessalonians with what he said to the Ephesians, it appeared on the surface that Paul himself was just a little confused. Writing to the Thessalonians, he called it the breastplate of faith and love (1 Thess. 5:8). Yet to the Ephesians, he referred to it as the breastplate of righteousness (Eph. 6:14).

And did not Paul state to the people of Ephesus that it was the shield of faith (Eph. 6:16)? But to the Thessalonians he referred to it as the breastplate of faith and love (1 Thess. 5:8). Then I noticed that to the Ephesians Paul did not even mention love as a vital piece of the armour that I was to put on.

Comparing First Thessalonians with Ephesians, I saw clearly that Paul did not remain loyal to his Roman soldier symbolism throughout his writings. To him, it did not matter whether faith or righteousness was our breastplate. With all of this in mind, I realized that I needed to refurbish my position concerning the degree of importance that I placed upon understanding the armour of the Roman soldier.

Refurbishing

Refurbishing a subject is accomplished by reexamining the basic questions that we must ask and answer in order to bring clarity to the issue at hand. We must ask questions such as, What is this armour that we are to put on? What exactly is it to be used against? What does it protect? How is this armour to be used?

Due to the fact that Paul did not remain loyal to his Roman soldier symbolism throughout his writings, it may be time to downplay its importance, and doing so may allow us to turn our attention to the more important issue: discovering the true armour of God.

There is a simple procedure that will assist us to look beyond the soldier symbolism and find the true armour of God that we are to put on. This procedure requires that we remove the Roman soldier phrases from within this passage. For the sake of clarity only, let us remove the terms *your loins girt, breastplate, feet shod, shield, helmet,* and *the sword* and see what is left.

Removing the soldier phrases, the passage in Ephesians would read as follows:

EPHESIANS 6:13-17

13 **Wherefore take unto you the whole armour of God, that ye may be able to withstand in the evil day, and having done all, to stand.**

14 **Stand therefore, having . . . truth, and having . . . righteousness;**

15 **And . . . with . . . the gospel of peace;**

16 **Above all, taking . . . faith, wherewith ye shall be able to quench all the fiery darts of the wicked.**

17 **And take . . . salvation, and . . . the word of God.**

Once the soldier terms are removed, it suddenly becomes apparent that the armour we are to put on is the armour of truth, righteousness, the gospel of peace, faith, salvation, and the Word of God.

Stop for a moment and think. Is Paul asking the church at Ephesus to put on salvation? Is not this epistle written to people who are already saved? Yes! Listen to the first verse of this letter to the Ephesians: *"Paul, an apostle of Jesus Christ by the will of God, to the saints which are at Ephesus, and to the faithful in Christ Jesus"* (Eph. 1:1).

Why would Paul admonish Christians to put on salvation? Once you have accepted the Lord Jesus into your life, you are saved. But now Paul is telling us to put on salvation again. What's that all about?

Then consider the fact that Paul also encourages us to put on righteousness. If anyone understood that the moment you received Jesus as your Saviour, at that instant you were made the righteousness of God in Christ, Paul did. Righteousness by faith was the gospel that Paul preached throughout his three missionary journeys.

Stop for a moment and think, dear reader. Paul is not instructing saints to put on salvation every day, nor is he encouraging us to put on righteousness every day. If he were, and if you forgot to put them on, then you could go around all day not being saved or not being righteous. And we know that this is not possible if you are a Christian.

So then, if we are not to put on our salvation every day, what does Paul mean in our Ephesians passage when he tells us to put on salvation? He is simply instructing us to put on daily *what we know* about our salvation. We are being admonished to put on *what we know* about our righteousness. We are to put on what we know about the truth, what we know about our faith, and what we know about the gospel of peace and the Word of God.

We Are to Put On What We Know

Do you see it, dear reader? The armour that we are to put on is the armour of *Bible knowledge*. Paul is informing us that if we desire to win, we must put on what we know about our salvation. Then we are to use what we know about our salvation against the enemy as he endeavors to destroy us.

The armour that we are to put on is the armour of Bible knowledge.

Oh glory! We are to put on what we know about truth, righteousness, and faith. We are to put on what we know about our salvation, the gospel of peace, and the Word of God. When we have put on what we know about these issues and when we use our knowledge of these things properly, we will not be defeated by the wiles of the devil. His fiery darts will no longer carry out their destructive work in our lives. If we are to avoid becoming another casualty of this war, we must put on and properly use the true armour of God, which is simply Bible knowledge. Glory!

With this truth in mind, I revisited my formative years. Suddenly, things became clear. If I had been clothed with the whole armour of God, I could have defeated the *"extra-cookie"* thought. I could have subdued the *"copy-Straight-A-Mary's-exam"* thought, and I would have suppressed the entire potato chip scheme. For each of these thoughts violated the truth or, in other words, the Word of God.

Oh, how I wish that I had understood as a child the importance of putting on the whole armour of God! So many problems—not to mention lectures and visits to the principal's office—could have been avoided.

Truth, the Gospel of Peace, and the Word of God

One day while reading Paul's admonishment to put on the whole armour of God, I suddenly focused on three specific issues—truth (Eph. 6:14), the gospel of peace (Eph. 6:15), and the Word of God (Eph. 6:17). As you consider these three carefully, may I present this thought for your consideration: Are they not the same? What is the difference between the truth and the Word of God? What is the difference between the Word of God and the gospel of peace? There is no difference!

Finally, I had what I needed to bring clarity to Paul's admonishment to put on the whole armour of God. Our armour that God has supplied us with is knowledge—Bible knowledge. Paul is simply encouraging us to put on and use what we know. Doing so will enable us to win each conflict that we encounter throughout our day. On the other hand, Paul strongly implies that if we fail to put on and use what we know, we will experience defeat—we will suffer the consequences of losing the battles within the mind.

Therefore, it seems clear: the quality of our life will be determined by how much we know and how well we use what we know. How well we use what we know about our salvation, faith, righteousness, the truth, the gospel of peace, and the Word of God in essence determines whether we win or lose this battle that Paul speaks of.

The Purpose Behind Using the Roman Soldier Symbolism

With all of this in mind, why did Paul use the Roman soldier symbolism in his Ephesians passage? I believe it was to drive home the severity of this battle—to paint a picture within us of the seriousness of this conflict. Paul wanted us to see that if we choose not to put on the "whole armour of God," we will experience defeat as quickly as would a soldier without armour in the midst of a battle.

Paul used the image of a soldier to impress upon us that we are not playing some childhood game. The consequences of not putting on the whole armour of God are real, and the quality of our life will diminish significantly should we lose this battle.

I don't know about you dear reader, but Paul got my attention with his symbolism.

CHAPTER 2

Knowledge and Its Proper Use Wins Battles

Wherefore take unto you the whole armour of God, that ye may be able to withstand in the evil day, and having done all, to stand.

Stand therefore, having . . . truth, and having . . . righteousness;

And . . . with . . . the gospel of peace;

Above all, taking . . . faith, wherewith ye shall be able to quench all the fiery darts of the wicked.

And take . . . salvation, and . . . the word of God.

—EPHESIANS 6:13-17

From the previous chapter, we discovered that the true armour of God is Bible knowledge. Paul encouraged us to put on what we know about the truth, righteousness, and the gospel of peace. In addition, we saw that we need to put on what we know about faith, salvation, and the Word of God. Doing so complies with Paul's admonishment to put on the whole armour of God. In essence, what Paul is declaring to us is that *knowledge and its proper use is the key to victory*. In other words, *knowledge and its proper use wins battles*. Therefore, it is only logical to conclude that when we experience defeat, the probable cause is either ignorance or a failure to use what we know properly.

Ignorance and Victory
Are Impossible Roommates

Since knowledge and its proper use wins battles, the opposite must also be true: ignorance and victory are impossible roommates. The person who is ignorant—the person who lacks knowledge about his salvation, his righteousness, or the Word of God—is standing in a battlefield wearing no armour. That person is easy prey for our enemy. Surprisingly, the Bible has much to say about the relationship between ignorance and defeat.

Hosea 4:6

For example, Hosea 4:6 says, *"My people are destroyed for lack of knowledge: because thou hast rejected knowledge,*

I will also reject thee, that thou shalt be no priest to me: seeing thou hast forgotten the law of thy God, I will also forget thy children."

The word "destroyed" is a combat term. It summarizes the condition of a person after they have lost a conflict. In other words, a battle raged, they lost, and they were ultimately destroyed by their enemy.

According to Hosea, the lack of knowledge permits destruction to gain access into our life. He implies that ignorance is not strong enough to protect us from destruction. On the other hand, it appears that Hosea is also implying that if God's people embrace knowledge and use it properly, they can avoid being destroyed. The truth seems clear: victory and ignorance are impossible roommates.

Isaiah 5:13

Another passage that establishes the principle that ignorance opens the door to failure and defeat is Isaiah 5:13: *"Therefore my people are gone into captivity, because they have no knowledge: and their honourable men are famished, and their multitude dried up with thirst."*

In Hosea, we were informed that we are *destroyed* because of a lack of knowledge. Through Isaiah, we now learn that we are taken *into captivity* because we "have no knowledge."

Similar to the word "destroyed" is the word "captivity." Again, it is battle terminology. Captivity implies that a battle raged, the individual lost, and they were ultimately carried off into captivity.

Once again, we find that the lack of knowledge is no defense during a time of war. No wonder Paul instructs us to put on the whole armour of God! Ignorance and victory are impossible roommates!

Knowledge and Its Proper Use Wins Battles

It is evident that ignorance cannot stop you from being destroyed or taken captive. But knowledge can! This implies that the person who lacks knowledge of the truth, their salvation, their righteousness, or their faith will be found allowing thoughts into their life that, if embraced, will lead them into captivity and destruction. But the person who knows that he is righteous and saved and who knows the Word of God will not embrace just any thought. We must allow God to clothe us with His truth, and if we will properly use what He has taught us, we can win the battles within our mind.

Luke provides an example of winning through the proper use of knowledge. In Luke chapter 4, we find the devil confronting Jesus in the wilderness. This passage shows our Lord Jesus putting on the armour of knowledge and using it to protect Himself when confronted by the devil.

LUKE 4:1-14

1 And Jesus being full of the Holy Ghost returned from Jordan, and was led by the Spirit into the wilderness,

2 Being forty days tempted of the devil. And in those days he did eat nothing: and when they were ended, he afterward hungered.

3 And the devil said unto him, If thou be the Son of God, command this stone that it be made bread.

4 And Jesus answered him, saying, It is written, That man shall not live by bread alone, but by every word of God.

5 And the devil, taking him up into an high mountain, shewed unto him all the kingdoms of the world in a moment of time.

6 And the devil said unto him, All this power will I give thee, and the glory of them: for that is delivered unto me; and to whomsoever I will I give it.

7 If thou therefore wilt worship me, all shall be thine.

8 And Jesus answered and said unto him, Get thee behind me, Satan: for it is written, Thou shalt worship the Lord thy God, and him only shalt thou serve.

9 And he brought him to Jerusalem, and set him on a pinnacle of the temple, and said unto him, If thou be the Son of God, cast thyself down from hence:

10 For it is written, He shall give his angels charge over thee, to keep thee:

11 And in their hands they shall bear thee up,
lest at any time thou dash thy foot against a
stone.

12 And Jesus answering said unto him, It is
said, Thou shalt not tempt the Lord thy God.

13 And when the devil had ended all the temp-
tation, he departed from him for a season.

14 And Jesus returned in the power of the
Spirit into Galilee: and there went out a
fame of him through all the region round
about.

This conflict began with the simple words spoken by
the devil, "If thou be the Son of God . . . ." Each time
Jesus was confronted by His enemy, He drove him back
with the use of His knowledge of the Word of God. Jesus
won His first encounter by saying, ". . . *It is written, That
man shall not live by bread alone, but by every word of
God*" (v. 4). The second time He prevailed by saying,
". . . *Get thee behind me, Satan: for it is written, Thou
shalt worship the Lord thy God, and him only shalt thou
serve*" (v. 8). Lastly, Jesus boldly proclaimed, ". . . *It is
said, Thou shalt not tempt the Lord thy God*" (v. 12).

What would have happened if Jesus had lacked

*Jesus exemplified for
us how to take unto
ourselves the whole
armour of God and
defeat the devil.*

Bible knowledge concerning the
issues that the devil presented
to him? He would have succumbed to the suggestions of the
wicked one. He would have lost
the confrontation. But He did

not lose; He did not become a casualty. Rather, He put on His armour of Bible knowledge and used it properly. Jesus exemplified for us how to take unto ourselves the whole armour of God and defeat the devil.

Jesus stated it plainly in John 8:32: *"And ye shall know the truth, and the truth shall make you free."* "Make you free" is once again combat terminology. Knowing the truth and properly using what we know will set us *free*!

According to Jesus, freedom was the direct result of knowledge. No wonder Paul prayed in Ephesians that the eyes of our understanding be enlightened (Eph. 1:16-18). No wonder pastors have been commissioned to feed the flock of God the Word of God (Acts 20:28). Unenlightened, untaught Christians are easily defeated by our enemy!

Consider This . . .

Knowledge and its proper use wins battles! Tucked within this phrase is this thought: the depth, height, length, and width of what we know of the Word of God will determine the depth, height, length, and width of our freedom. Small amount of Bible knowledge—small amount of freedom. The more we know, the more victory we can enjoy. This principle is also true concerning natural things: the more we know in the natural, the more we will be able to enjoy life.

Therefore, I encourage you to dedicate yourself today to a life of learning. Determine from this day forward to place great value on learning from the Word. Our desire to learn must be a driving force within our life.

Once again, the degree of victory we experience in our life will be in direct proportion to the amount of Bible knowledge that we possess and use properly.

Knowledge and its proper use wins battles!

CHAPTER 3

The Weapons of Our Enemy

Finally, my brethren, be strong in the Lord, and in the power of his might.

Put on the whole armour of God, that ye may be able to stand against the wiles of the devil.

For we wrestle not against flesh and blood, but against principalities, against powers, against the rulers of the darkness of this world, against spiritual wickedness in high places.

Wherefore take unto you the whole armour of God, that ye may be able to withstand in the evil day, and having done all, to stand.

Stand therefore, having your loins girt about with truth, and having on the breastplate of righteousness;

And your feet shod with the preparation of the gospel of peace;

> *Above all, taking the shield of faith, wherewith*
> *ye shall be able to quench all the fiery darts of the*
> *wicked.*
>
> *And take the helmet of salvation, and the*
> *sword of the Spirit, which is the word of God.*
>
> *—EPHESIANS 6:10-17*

The true armour of God is truth, righteousness, the gospel of peace, faith, salvation, and the Word of God. Therefore, we must conclude that our armour is simply *what we know* about these issues.

We increase our ability to enjoy victory in the midst of a conflict as we increase our knowledge about these subjects. Should ignorance reign in our life, we should not be surprised if we find ourselves losing this conflict that Paul speaks of.

Moving On

Now that we understand what our armour really is, the obvious question arises: What are we to use the armour of our Bible knowledge against? According to the Apostle Paul, we are to use our armour against three things: *the wiles of the devil* (Eph. 6:11), *the evil day* (Eph. 6:13), and *all the fiery darts of the wicked* (Eph. 6:16).

The wiles, the evil day, and the fiery darts all come from our enemy the devil, who is out to steal, kill, and destroy us (John 10:10). But we can take great comfort in knowing that as we take our Bible knowledge and use it properly, there will not be one wile, evil day, or fiery dart hurled at us that we cannot defeat. We can win every time if we put on and properly use the armour that our loving Heavenly Father has provided for us. Glory!

Our Enemy Is Predictable

Our enemy has had the advantage for too long because we lack understanding of where and how he will attack.

So many believers today are unaware of the battleground and of exactly what weapons their enemy will use in his attack. Our enemy has had the advantage for too long because we lack understanding of where and how he will attack.

In Second Corinthians 2:11 Paul says, *"Lest Satan should get an advantage of us: for we are not ignorant of his devices."* Apparently, Paul was not ignorant of the devil's devices. Apparently, he knew what our enemy would use in his attack. And if Paul knew, then we also can know.

The tactics of the devil are not a secret. We can know where he will attack and how he will attack. His approach is the same toward all, and all can know the weapons he uses. His mode of operation never changes.

He is not a creative being. He does not come up with new ideas and ways to inflict mankind from generation to generation. In other words, our enemy is knowable and predictable.

Identifying the Battle

So the question remains, What are we to use our armour against? What does our enemy hurl at us? What exactly are the wiles, evil day, and fiery darts? I present this for your consideration: they are thoughts, ideas, and suggestions.

When I discovered this truth, I shouted for joy! I suddenly began to realize that this armour of Bible knowledge equips us to win the battle within the mind. Our armour is the equipment that we must use in order to maintain our thought life. In other words, we are to use what we know about the truth, righteousness, the gospel of peace, faith, salvation, and the Word of God to win the battle within our mind.

The confrontation with thoughts, ideas, and suggestions is an unavoidable battle. We will be engaged in this battle for the rest of our life. Therefore, our diligence to maintain our thought life will directly determine the quality of our life in every arena.

If we fail to maintain our minds—if we fail to guard our thought life—we will find ourselves living on a level of life that is inferior to what our Heavenly Father desires for us, His children.

For example, the deterioration of a marriage relationship begins when either the husband or the wife fails to properly maintain their thoughts about their spouse. Rebellion toward parents gains access in a teenager as thoughts are entertained that should have been resisted long ago.

Individuals who are obsessed with pornography are showing proof that they have not maintained their thought life properly. When depression, fear, and discouragement dominate a child of God, it reveals their failure to maintain their thought life properly.

Some would lead us to believe that the remedy for these issues is to have hands laid upon us in a church service. As believers, we must understand that the prayer line is not to be used as a cure-all. The benefits of a prayer line are limited. In the New Testament, we find specific uses for the laying on of hands. For example, it is used when ministering to the sick (Mark 16:17,18). The laying on of hands is also used to send out ministers into their ministry (Acts 13:1-3). In the Book of Acts, we find the laying on of hands used to administer to fellow believers the baptism of the Holy Spirit with the evidence of speaking with other tongues (Acts 19:1-6). Also, Jesus laid His hands on little children to bless them (Mark 10:15,16).

Nowhere in the Bible do we find the laying on of hands used to release a person from depression or discouragement. Nowhere do we find the laying on of hands used to administer freedom from lust or worry. We must understand that the laying on of hands is not a cure-all for every pollutant that men allow into their lives. There are some areas that demand the maintenance of the mind in order to experience victory.

We are in a battle and it is primarily fought in the arena of the mind. Lives hang in the balance. Marriages stand at risk. The advancement of the Kingdom of God is in jeopardy. We must be clear in our thinking as to who our enemy is, where he will attack, and what weapons he will use. In this chapter, I have but suggested that the darts he hurls at us are thoughts, ideas, and suggestions. In the next chapter, I will provide sound evidence that will prove beyond doubt that the weapons our enemy uses against us are thoughts, ideas, and suggestions. We must not be ignorant of his devices.

The Battlefield Is the Mind

Can we be certain that the weapons of our enemy which we are to use our armour against are thoughts, ideas, and suggestions? Can we be certain that the target of our enemy is our mind? Can we be certain that thoughts, ideas, and suggestions are the fiery darts that Paul is speaking of in his letter to the Ephesians? Absolutely yes!

No matter the type of war that is fought, winning depends upon knowing your enemy. Knowledge of their strengths, weaknesses, weapons, and methods of attack are vital if victory is to be expected. This principle holds true concerning our conflict with the devil himself. The more we know about him, the easier it is to stand against him. Therefore, it becomes necessary to observe the devil's method of attack in previous battles with mankind throughout the Word of God. Who he was able to destroy, or not able to destroy, is not the issue. His

method of attack is what we are looking to discover.
Once known, he becomes predictable. Once we know
him, we then know where he will attack, and how, giving us the advantage. The following conflicts and verses
will reveal clearly that what the devil uses against us
are nothing more than thoughts, ideas, and suggestions,
and his target is our mind.

Precedence

In Genesis chapter 3, we find a precedent-setting
event. Generally speaking, a precedent is a record of an
act that acts as a guide for future acts of a similar kind.
Any time something is allowed to happen for the first
time, it sets precedent. For example, there are court
cases that have been sent before our Supreme Court
that we seek to defeat. The reason is, if these cases are
approved, they would set such precedent that society as
a whole would be negatively impacted. In other words, if
the Supreme Court allows a group of people to behave
in a certain manner, then it must allow anyone else who
comes after them to repeat the identical activity
because the precedent has been set.

In Genesis, we have the account of the devil
approaching man for the first time. Therefore, this
account is classified as a precedent-setting event. It
serves as a guide for future acts of a similar kind.

Observing the devil's method of attack toward Eve in
the Garden of Eden will assist us in discovering how he

will attack us today. If we discover how he defeated her, we can learn how he will endeavor to defeat us. What he used to defeat her will be what he uses in his endeavors to defeat us. Let's look into this precedent-setting event.

GENESIS 3:1-6

1 Now the serpent was more subtil than any beast of the field which the Lord God had made. And he said unto the woman, Yea, hath God said, Ye shall not eat of every tree of the garden?

2 And the woman said unto the serpent, We may eat of the fruit of the trees of the garden:

3 But of the fruit of the tree which is in the midst of the garden, God hath said, Ye shall not eat of it, neither shall ye touch it, lest ye die.

4 And the serpent said unto the woman, Ye shall not surely die:

5 For God doth know that in the day ye eat thereof, then your eyes shall be opened, and ye shall be as gods, knowing good and evil.

6 And when the woman saw that the tree was good for food, and that it was pleasant to the eyes, and a tree to be desired to make one wise, she took of the fruit thereof, and did eat, and gave also unto her husband with her; and he did eat.

As we consider this passage, something emerges that has escaped detection in the past—something unexpected. Notice as we observe the devil approaching Eve that he does not approach her fiercely. In his approach, he does not frighten her with his presence. Signs of his might and power are not visible. In other words, contrary to popular belief, Eve is not frightened by him. The absence of fear during this encounter is a notable fact.

Since this is a precedent-setting event—since it acts as a guide for future acts of a similar kind—could it be possible, as the enemy approaches us today, that he will not come with mighty displays of his power and viciousness? Could it be possible that as he approaches us, he will not exhibit his fierceness in hopes of causing us to tremble uncontrollably? Therefore, could it be possible that we have come to improper conclusions concerning the general atmosphere surrounding a personal encounter with the devil himself? I believe we have.

The Attack

Listen carefully as the devil initiates his attack toward Eve. It begins in Genesis 3:1: *"Now the serpent was more subtil than any beast of the field which the Lord God had made. And he said unto the woman, Yea, hath God said, Ye shall not eat of every tree of the garden?"*

The attack begins with little fanfare, and not one sign of the devil's evil intent to ultimately destroy Eve is evident. His approach is full of deception, almost giving the impression that he is a friend whose only desire is that Eve enjoy everything that will enhance her personal life. The first thought that he tosses gently toward Eve is reasonable. He simply asks, *"Yea, hath God said, Ye shall not eat of every tree of the garden?"*

Notice that Eve's reply contains no evidence that she is aware of any prevailing danger, and the presence of fear is nowhere to be found. She replies, *". . . We may eat of the fruit of the trees of the garden: But of the fruit of the tree which is in the midst of the garden, God hath said, Ye shall not eat of it, neither shall ye touch it, lest ye die"* (vv. 2,3).

The devil's response was calm, cool, and collected, even though he knew that he was leading her into destruction: *". . . Ye shall not surely die: For God doth know that in the day ye eat thereof, then your eyes shall be opened, and ye shall be as gods, knowing good and evil"* (vv. 4,5).

The possibilities of her eyes being opened, becoming as a god, and knowing both good and evil were attractive to Eve. She had not considered such options before. The suggested possibilities, previously unknown to her, seemed now well within her reach. She considered the suggestions, and we are all too familiar with the outcome. She entertained and embraced the suggestions, partook of the forbidden fruit, and you know "the rest of the story."

With all of this in mind, remember: we are currently seeking the answer to the questions raised at the beginning of this chapter. Can we be certain that what the enemy hurls at us are thoughts, ideas, and suggestions? Can we be certain that where our enemy attacks us—in other words, the battlefield—is within the mental arena? Can we be certain that thoughts, ideas, and suggestions are the fiery darts that Paul is speaking of in his letter to the Ephesians?

From our first piece of evidence found in Genesis 3:1-6, it is clear that the devil used thoughts, ideas, and suggestions in his endeavors against Eve. He used thoughts such as, *"Yea, hath God said, Ye shall not eat of every tree of the garden?"* Again, he presented the idea, *"Ye shall not surely die."* And lastly, he offered this thought: *"For God doth know that in the day ye eat thereof, then your eyes shall be opened, and ye shall be as gods, knowing good and evil."*

This precedent-setting event clearly reveals how and where he will attack us. It also reveals that his attack will be accompanied by a degree of calmness that will not trigger a sense of danger within us. His arsenal will be thoughts, ideas, and suggestions. They will sound as if they are leading us into a better life with more possibilities. But where they will ultimately lead us is where despair and defeat make their home. They will be logical and reasonable thoughts which, if embraced, will lead us away from our loving Heavenly Father.

It is obvious that this conflict took place within Eve's mind, and what the devil hurled at her were thoughts, ideas, and suggestions. Had she maintained her thought life, she would not have succumbed to the enemy. Therefore, we must learn from the mistakes of those who have gone before us. We must understand the importance of maintaining our thought life.

As we evaluate our enemy's attack on Eve, it becomes clear that the wiles, evil day, and fiery darts are nothing more than thoughts, ideas, and suggestions.

The Second Piece of Evidence

We are examining our enemy's past in order to discover his pattern of attack and the devices that he uses today. In Luke chapter 4, we find another occasion where our enemy used thoughts, ideas, and suggestions in his attack. This time his target is our Lord Jesus. The more we discover and know about our enemy, the more predictable he becomes.

LUKE 4:1-13

1   **And Jesus being full of the Holy Ghost returned from Jordan, and was led by the Spirit into the wilderness,**

2   **Being forty days tempted of the devil. And in those days he did eat nothing: and when they were ended, he afterward hungered.**

3   **And the devil said unto him, If thou be the Son of God, command this stone that it be made bread.**

4   **And Jesus answered him, saying, It is written, That man shall not live by bread alone, but by every word of God.**

5   And the devil, taking him up into an high
mountain, shewed unto him all the kingdoms of the world in a moment of time.

6   And the devil said unto him, All this power
will I give thee, and the glory of them: for
that is delivered unto me; and to whomsoever
I will I give it.

7   If thou therefore wilt worship me, all shall
be thine.

8   And Jesus answered and said unto him, Get
thee behind me, Satan: for it is written, Thou
shalt worship the Lord thy God, and him
only shalt thou serve.

9   And he brought him to Jerusalem, and set
him on a pinnacle of the temple, and said
unto him, If thou be the Son of God, cast thyself down from hence:

10 For it is written, He shall give his angels
charge over thee, to keep thee:

11 And in their hands they shall bear thee up,
lest at any time thou dash thy foot against a
stone.

12 And Jesus answering said unto him, It is
said, Thou shalt not tempt the Lord thy God.

13 And when the devil had ended all the temp-
tation, he departed from him for a season.

While in the wilderness, Jesus comes into contact
with the devil. As the devil closes in on Jesus, it seems
evident that the tone of his approach, his attitude, and
the weapons that he uses are almost a carbon copy of

the attack on Eve in the Garden of Eden. His attack is calculated and clearly premeditated as to how he will deploy his arsenal. And what again is surprising is the absence of fear throughout this entire encounter.

Exactly as in his approach to Eve, the devil uses thoughts, ideas, and suggestions in his endeavors to defeat Jesus. The thoughts used are not repulsive or dismaying; rather, they are reasonable, logical thoughts. They give no hint of their hidden design to defeat Jesus and render Him powerless to accomplish God's will.

The devil offered simple thoughts such as, ". . . *If thou be the Son of God, command this stone that it be made bread*" (v. 3). After taking Jesus onto a high mountain, the devil showed him all the kingdoms of the world and then whispered, ". . . *All this power will I give thee, and the glory of them: for that is delivered unto me; and to whomsoever I will I give it. If thou therefore wilt worship me, all shall be thine*" (vv. 6,7). Afterward, the devil brought Jesus to Jerusalem and set him on a pinnacle of the temple and offered to him the suggestion, ". . . *If thou be the Son of God, cast thyself down from hence: For it is written, He shall give his angels charge over thee, to keep thee: And in their hands they shall bear thee up, lest at any time thou dash thy foot against a stone*" (vv. 9-11).

Clearly conclusive through this encounter is the fact that when Jesus encountered the devil's wiles, evil day, and fiery darts, they came in the form of thoughts, ideas, and suggestions. But Jesus took what He knew and used it to defend Himself, and He defeated the enemy on each occasion. He did that by maintaining His thought life. He won because He used His armour properly. Knowledge and its proper use wins battles. Glory!

Eve, on the other hand, was attacked by the same wiles, yet she failed to use what knowledge she had and lost her conflict with the enemy. She failed to maintain her thought life, embraced the suggestions offered to her, and was easily defeated. She became the first human casualty of this war that Paul speaks of in Ephesians. She failed to put on the armour that God had given her and use it properly.

The Third Piece of Evidence

The third passage that must be considered when establishing the fact that what the devil uses against us is thoughts, ideas, and suggestions is found in the Gospel of John.

John 8:44 says, *"Ye are of your father the devil, and the lusts of your father ye will do. He was a murderer from the beginning, and abode not in the truth, because there is no truth in him. When he speaketh a lie, he speaketh of his own: for he is a liar, and the father of it."*

The devil is a liar! His lies are offered to us through thoughts, ideas, and suggestions. His false impressions many times will come without any sense of danger attached to them. They are lies containing just enough truth that the casual Christian will spend too little time to examine them completely. But like a Trojan horse, the devil's thought contains deadly consequences should the lie be embraced.

We have learned from looking at our enemy's activities with Eve and Jesus that the weapons he uses to attack man are thoughts, ideas, and suggestions. Now John further verifies these findings by informing us that the devil is nothing but a liar.

> *. . . like a Trojan horse, the devil's thought contains deadly consequences should the lie be embraced.*

The Fourth Piece of Evidence

The fourth passage that should be considered as proof that the weapons the devil uses are thoughts, ideas, and suggestions is located in the Book of Revelation.

In Revelation chapter 12, we find a very interesting passage that gives further insight into the operations of our enemy.

REVELATION 12:7-9

7   **And there was war in heaven: Michael and his angels fought against the dragon; and the dragon fought and his angels,**

8   **And prevailed not; neither was their place found any more in heaven.**

9   **And the great dragon was cast out, that old serpent, called the Devil, and Satan, which**

**deceiveth the whole world: he was cast out
into the earth, and his angels were cast out
with him.**

Nestled within this account is a phrase that reveals
much about the activity of our enemy. Notice the last
verse: *"And the great dragon was cast out, that old serpent, called the Devil, and Satan, WHICH DECEIVETH
THE WHOLE WORLD: he was cast out into the earth,
and his angels were cast out with him"* (v. 9).

The phrase *". . . which deceiveth the whole world . . ."*
is a statement of summary. It summarizes the activities
of the devil upon the earth. His mission is to deceive us.
The word "deceive" implies *to cause us to think on
things that are not true.* Therefore, ultimately the devil
is out to cause us to think on things that are not true.
And the devices that he uses to deceive us are nothing
more than thoughts, ideas, and suggestions. Through
the use of thoughts, ideas, and suggestions, he attempts
to lure us into thinking on things that are not true.

Let's review. The devil successfully deceived Eve
(1 Tim. 2:14). He unsuccessfully tried to deceive Jesus.
John's Gospel refers to him as a liar, and now John
describes him as a deceiver in Revelation chapter 12.

But there is an additional piece of evidence to support our conclusion that what our enemy uses against
us are thoughts, ideas, and suggestions. The following
passage from Revelation chapter 20 speaks of a future
event that will be glorious. It is one that all of God's

people look forward to with great anticipation. Let's read it first and then we will draw from it a few nuggets of truth.

REVELATION 20:1-10

1 And I saw an angel come down from heaven, having the key of the bottomless pit and a great chain in his hand.

2 And he laid hold on the dragon, that old serpent, which is the Devil, and Satan, and bound him a thousand years,

3 And cast him into the bottomless pit, and shut him up, and set a seal upon him, that he should deceive the nations no more, till the thousand years should be fulfilled: and after that he must be loosed a little season.

4 And I saw thrones, and they sat upon them, and judgment was given unto them: and I saw the souls of them that were beheaded for the witness of Jesus, and for the word of God, and which had not worshipped the beast, neither his image, neither had received his mark upon their foreheads, or in their hands; and they lived and reigned with Christ a thousand years.

5 But the rest of the dead lived not again until the thousand years were finished. This is the first resurrection.

6 Blessed and holy is he that hath part in the first resurrection: on such the second death hath no power, but they shall be priests of God and of Christ, and shall reign with him a thousand years.

7 And when the thousand years are expired,
Satan shall be loosed out of his prison,

8 And shall go out to deceive the nations
which are in the four quarters of the earth,
Gog and Magog, to gather them together to
battle: the number of whom is as the sand of
the sea.

9 And they went up on the breadth of the
earth, and compassed the camp of the saints
about, and the beloved city: and fire came
down from God out of heaven, and devoured
them.

10 And the devil that deceived them was cast
into the lake of fire and brimstone, where
the beast and the false prophet are, and
shall be tormented day and night for ever
and ever.

According to this passage there is coming a time—a
glorious time—when the devil will be bound with a
chain by an angel from God. He will then be cast into
the bottomless pit and a seal will be placed upon him.
And notice the words in verse three: *". . . that he should
deceive the nations no more, till the thousand years
should be fulfilled: and after that he must be loosed a
little season."*

Here again we find the familiar phrase, *". . . that he
should deceive the nations no more."* Keeping in mind
this phrase and our passage from Revelation chapter 12,
we can draw a clear conclusion. That conclusion is this:
During every loosed moment the devil has upon this

earth until he is bound and placed into the bottomless pit for a thousand years, he will be about the business of deceiving. He will be about the business of causing us to think on things that are not true. And he accomplishes his business through the use of thoughts, ideas, and suggestions.

Now the question arises, What will the devil do when he is loosed after the thousand years? The answer is found in Revelation chapter 20.

REVELATION 20:7,8

7 And when the thousand years are expired, Satan shall be loosed out of his prison,

8 And shall go out to deceive the nations which are in the four quarters of the earth, Gog and Magog, to gather them together to battle: the number of whom is as the sand of the sea.

The Bible informs us that after the devil is loosed from his thousand-year imprisonment, he will *"go out to deceive the nations which are in the four quarters of the earth."*

The final analysis is clear: during every loosed moment the devil has upon this earth, he is about the business of deceiving mankind. His mission is to cause us to think on things that are not true, trusting that we will eventually embrace his deceptive thoughts. Only then does he gain access into our lives.

Considering the Evidence

Having considered these scriptural accounts as evidence, let us return to the questions which were presented at the beginning of this chapter. Can we be certain that what the enemy hurls at us are thoughts, ideas, and suggestions? Can we be certain that where our enemy attacks us is within the mental arena? Can we be certain that thoughts, ideas, and suggestions are the fiery darts that Paul is speaking of in his letter to the Ephesians?

Let us take into consideration the devil's approaches toward Eve in Genesis chapter 3 and Jesus in Luke chapter 4; Jesus' words in John chapter 8; and John's statements in Revelation chapters 12 and 20. As we do, we can clearly see that our enemy uses thoughts, ideas, and suggestions in his endeavors to conquer us.

Now that we know what the devil uses against us, let us return to a verse that was mentioned in the previous chapter. Second Corinthians 2:11 says, *"Lest Satan should get an advantage of us: for we are not ignorant of his devices."* Like Paul, we also may now say that we are not ignorant of Satan's devices. His devices are thoughts, ideas, and suggestions. And the devil uses these devices to attack our mind.

If all that we have stated thus far is true, then it is imperative that we learn how to maintain our thought life if we are going to enjoy Christian success. If we are to remain moral and upright in this world, and if we are to ensure strong marriages, we must maintain our thought life. If we are to obtain the promises of healing and godly blessings through faith, we must understand the importance of maintaining our thought life. If victory is our goal, then the maintenance of our thought life must of necessity be our constant duty.

What are the wiles that we are to stand against, enabled by our armour? What is the evil day that we are encouraged to withstand, empowered by our armour? What are the fiery darts that we are to quench with the armour of God? If observing our enemy throughout his past teaches us anything, it teaches us that these things are nothing more than thoughts, ideas, and suggestions. And the battlefield within which we confront our enemy is our mind.

Knowing such things as what the war is, where it will be fought, what devices our enemy will use against us, and what armour we are to put on in order for us to win brings much comfort to our souls. Such knowledge is empowering! It energizes us with an expectation that allows us to believe that we can win this battle. Victory seems to be within our reach, when for so long it seemed so far away. Jesus knew what He was talking about when He said, *"And ye shall know the truth, and the truth shall make you free"* (John 8:32). Glory to God!

A Look Into the Past to Understand the Present

Before we begin to examine how we are to protect our mind with our armour of Bible knowledge, there is one small truth that we must not neglect. It is found in Peter's writings.

1 PETER 5:8

8   Be sober, be vigilant; because your adversary the devil, as a roaring lion, walketh about, seeking whom he may devour.

Peter reveals that our adversary walks about seeking whom he *may* devour. The obvious question that arises is, Who is it that he *may* devour? Knowing that our enemy uses thoughts, ideas, and suggestions against us, we can see the answer clearly: he may devour those who have failed to maintain their thought life.

> *Our adversary the devil walks about seeking those who have neglected to vigilantly maintain their thought life.*

Our adversary the devil walks about seeking those who have neglected to vigilantly maintain their thought life. This conclusion becomes obvious as we once again review the activities of our adversary as seen throughout the Word of God.

Eve

The first person who the devil devoured was Eve. As we saw in the previous chapter, Eve was presented with a series of thoughts, such as, *"Yea, hath God said, Ye shall not eat of every tree of the garden?"* She replies, *"We may eat of the fruit of the trees of the garden: but of the fruit of the tree which is in the midst of the garden, God hath said, Ye shall not eat of it, neither shall ye touch it, lest ye die"* (Gen. 3:1-3).

The devil's response was, *"Ye shall not surely die: For God doth know that in the day ye eat thereof, then your eyes shall be opened, and ye shall be as gods, knowing good and evil"* (Gen. 3:4,5).

Embracing the thoughts presented to her, Eve partakes of the forbidden fruit. Immediately a change occurs within her. She now knows that she is naked, and when God calls out for her, she finds herself running from His presence—something she has never done before. Clearly, she has fallen from her place in God; she has been devoured because she failed to maintain her thought life properly.

God's original intention for Eve was that she enjoy her fellowship with Him and that she enjoy the garden He had provided. But she failed to guard her thought life properly, and the result was that she fell from God's best. Clearly, the devil was walking about seeking whom he might devour and found Eve as a prime candidate.

Eve fell from her position in God because she did not maintain her thought life. I wonder how many husbands and wives have fallen below the position and place that God intended for them in the marriage relationship because they did not maintain their thought life properly? I wonder how many relationships between children and their parents have been damaged because of thoughts that were embraced over time that should have been rejected the first time they were presented? I wonder how many dear saints have failed to obtain physical healing because they failed to take a vigilant enough stance against the doubts that kept coming to them about the outcome of their situation?

If we learn and glean from the mistake of Eve, we should be more aware that we must vigilantly watch over our thought life. For the devil walks about as a roaring lion seeking whom he may devour.

Judas Iscariot

As we endeavor to discover what type of people the devil *may* devour, the second person who comes to mind is Judas Iscariot. Along with Matthew, Andrew, James, and John, Judas was one of the twelve apostles. These handpicked men were being personally trained and groomed by our Lord Jesus to carry on after His departure. During this time of training, the devil approached Judas. In the devil's hand was nothing more than an idea. This idea if embraced would ultimately escort Judas into an action that would eventually abort the call of God upon his life.

John 13:2 says, *"And supper being ended, the devil having now put into the heart of Judas Iscariot, Simon's son, to betray him."* Apparently, it was the devil's intent to influence Judas to do something that Judas would never have thought of on his own. The idea presented to Judas was to betray the Lord Jesus. For whatever reason, Judas failed to vigilantly watch over what he allowed himself to consider. This failure was the door that allowed the devil access into his life. It allowed the devil such access that after Judas acted upon the thought, he slipped away in shame and hanged himself.

The obvious conclusion to this matter was that the devil walked into the life of Judas through the door of his mind. His life and future were bright, but he failed to bridle his mind and he fell from his place—he fell from his grace. Oh, the misery that we could avoid if only we would maintain our thought life properly!

First Peter 5:8 says, *"Be sober, be vigilant; because your adversary the devil, as a roaring lion, walketh about, seeking whom he may devour."* Whom may the devil devour? Considering Eve and Judas, it appears that the devil may devour those who fail to maintain their thought life. Wisdom learns from the mistakes of others. Therefore, be wise and learn.

Ananias and Sapphira

The third example that comes to mind as we consider the issue of who *may* the devil devour is that of Ananias and Sapphira. Their story is found in Acts chapter 5.

ACTS 5:1-11

1 **But a certain man named Ananias, with Sapphira his wife, sold a possession,**

2 **And kept back part of the price, his wife also being privy to it, and brought a certain part, and laid it at the apostles' feet.**

3 **But Peter said, Ananias, why hath Satan filled thine heart to lie to the Holy Ghost, and to keep back part of the price of the land?**

4 **Whiles it remained, was it not thine own? and after it was sold, was it not in thine own power? why hast thou conceived this thing in thine heart? thou hast not lied unto men, but unto God.**

5 And Ananias hearing these words fell down, and gave up the ghost: and great fear came on all them that heard these things.

6 And the young men arose, wound him up, and carried him out, and buried him.

7 And it was about the space of three hours after, when his wife, not knowing what was done, came in.

8 And Peter answered unto her, Tell me whether ye sold the land for so much? And she said, Yea, for so much.

9 Then Peter said unto her, How is it that ye have agreed together to tempt the Spirit of the Lord? behold, the feet of them which have buried thy husband are at the door, and shall carry thee out.

10 Then fell she down straightway at his feet, and yielded up the ghost: and the young men came in, and found her dead, and, carrying her forth, buried her by her husband.

11 And great fear came upon all the church, and upon as many as heard these things.

The deaths of Ananias and Sapphira—what a tragic event! But why did they die? It is clear that they were devoured, that they fell from their place. But what was the cause? Peter's words recorded for us in verse 3 provide the answer: "*. . . why hath Satan filled thine heart to lie to the Holy Ghost . . . ?*" Apparently, Ananias and Sapphira allowed the devil to fill their hearts to lie. What did the devil use to accomplish this? He must have used a little thought, idea, or suggestion, such as, *"You would be better off to keep back part of the money. No one will ever know. Go ahead—sell the land, but keep some of the money for yourself. Then announce when you present your offering that you are giving all of it. That will really impress the leaders of the church and you will be esteemed highly."*

Such thoughts would imply to Ananias and Sapphira that their life would be enhanced if they would simply agree with the suggested thought. Instead, embracing those thoughts led them away from God and His provision, and eventually led them into death. The maintenance of our thought life is far more important than we have believed. From what we know of our enemy and the history of how he attacks, we can see clearly that Ananias and Sapphira were devoured because they did not maintain their thought life properly.

Eve, Judas, Ananias, and Sapphira were attacked by the devil, and each of them was devoured. In each case, all evidence points to the cause as being an improperly maintained thought life. Could this be the deciding factor in determining whom the devil may devour? Absolutely!

I trust I am painting a clear enough picture within you concerning the importance of our duty to maintain our thought life. This matter must be addressed. Our quality of life and effectiveness within this world have suffered greatly due to our lack of knowledge concerning this area. It's time for this subject to be brought to the attention of God-fearing saints.

The Devil Himself

As we consider Eve, Judas, Ananias, and Sapphira, we can see clearly that failure to maintain one's thought life can have disastrous results. Eventually, our lack of vigilance in this arena will cause us to fail. It will cause us to fall from our place and to fall from our grace.

As I continued my research into this subject, I unexpectedly discovered that the devil is also a prime example of someone falling from his God-intended position, and it is clear that the cause of his fall was his unbridled thought life.

The Bible also refers to the devil as Lucifer. He was at one time a very powerful angelic being. So powerful was he that he apparently had lesser angels assigned under his command. Together they were included among God's angelic host.

However, during his service to God, Lucifer began to think. He began to entertain thoughts. They have been recorded for us in Isaiah chapter 14. Read them carefully, for within them we find that Lucifer's downfall was the eventual result of his failure to maintain his thought life properly.

ISAIAH 14:12-17

12 How art thou fallen from heaven, O Lucifer, son of the morning! how art thou cut down

to the ground, which didst weaken the
nations!

13 For thou hast said in thine heart, I will
ascend into heaven, I will exalt my throne
above the stars of God: I will sit also upon
the mount of the congregation, in the sides
of the north:

14 I will ascend above the heights of the clouds;
I will be like the most High.

15 Yet thou shalt be brought down to hell, to
the sides of the pit.

16 They that see thee shall narrowly look upon
thee, and consider thee, saying, Is this the
man that made the earth to tremble, that did
shake kingdoms;

17 That made the world as a wilderness, and
destroyed the cities thereof; that opened not
the house of his prisoners?

The questions are clear: *"How art thou fallen from
heaven . . . ? How art thou cut down to the ground?"*
(v. 12). So many dear saints are being devoured today,
and it is so sad that only a minority ever ask why.

Isaiah supplies us with the answers to these questions about Lucifer, or the devil: *"I will ascend into
heaven, I will exalt my throne above the stars of God: I
will sit also upon the mount of the congregation, in the
sides of the north: I will ascend above the heights of the
clouds; I will be like the most High"* (vv. 13,14).

In other words, Lucifer had shown proof that he had
spent much time considering the possibilities of

dethroning God. For he had said in his heart, "I will ascend into heaven and I will exalt my throne above the stars of God. I will be like the Most High."

The passage in Isaiah continues, *"Yet thou shalt be brought down to hell, to the sides of the pit. They that see thee shall narrowly look upon thee, and consider thee, saying, Is this the man that made the earth to tremble, that did shake kingdoms; that made the world as a wilderness, and destroyed the cities thereof; that opened not the house of his prisoners"* (vv. 15-17)?

We know that Lucifer failed in his attempt to dethrone God. When Lucifer executed his plan, he exposed himself as an enemy of God and all that He stands for. We know that Lucifer was removed from his God-given position, and since that time he has remained God's archenemy.

But the more important lesson to be learned is that Lucifer's downfall was the result of his uncontrolled, unmaintained thought life—nothing more, nothing less. He allowed his mind to consider and embrace thoughts that would eventually lead him to his ruin. Those thoughts would render him incapable of enjoying the type of life and position that God originally intended for him.

The Devil Learned From His Mistakes

Now the devil may be God's enemy, but he is an intelligent enemy. After his defeat—after his plan failed—don't you know that the devil did some thinking! I can almost hear his little mind grind as he considered all the events that led up to his actual attempt to dethrone God. He must have realized that it all began with a thought. As he further considered what happened, his thoughts must have sounded something like this: *"Now wait a minute. If I fell because I did not maintain my thought life, then all those who fail to maintain their thought life will fall too."*

The devil had made a discovery, but he needed to experiment with this newfound principle. So he approached Eve, his first human target, and simply hurled some thoughts, ideas, and suggestions toward her. To his amazement, she embraced them and acted upon them, and down she fell. Eve fell from her position with God so easily that it must have surprised even the devil himself. She had proved his theory to be true. And ever since that encounter, the devil has been about the business of offering thoughts, ideas, and suggestions to anyone who will listen. For through his own demise, he learned that the unmaintained mind is the door that will lead a person into failure and ruin.

I present the following for your consideration. We know how Lucifer fell from his place. And we know how Eve, Judas, Ananias, and Sapphira were devoured by the devil. Therefore, would it not be logical to conclude that in order for us to live successful Christian lives today, we must guard, or maintain, our thought life? Absolutely!

The mind is the battlefield! No wonder Paul taught the church that they should be *"casting down imaginations, and every high thing that exalteth itself against the knowledge of God, and bringing into captivity every thought to the obedience of Christ"* (2 Cor. 10:5).

And to the Philippians Paul said, *"Finally, brethren, whatsoever things are true, whatsoever things are honest, whatsoever things are just, whatsoever things are pure, whatsoever things are lovely, whatsoever things are of good report; if there be any virtue, and if there be any praise, THINK ON THESE THINGS"* (Phil. 4:8).

Now that we understand whom the devil *may* devour, and we understand that what he hurls at us are thoughts, ideas, and suggestions, we have a foundation laid in order to understand the following.

Revelation 20:1-3 says, *"And I saw an angel come down from heaven, having the key of the bottomless pit and a great chain in his hand. And he laid hold on the dragon, that old serpent, which is the Devil, and Satan, and bound him a thousand years, and cast him into the bottomless pit, and shut him up, and set a seal upon him, THAT HE SHOULD DECEIVE THE NATIONS NO MORE, till the thousand years should be fulfilled: and after that he must be loosed a little season."*

Note the phrase "*. . . that he should deceive the nations no more,*" and notice what this verse does *not* say. It does not say "that he should cause divorce among couples no more." It does not say "that he should cause teenagers to rebel against their parents no more." Why? Because the root cause of all these outcomes is an unmaintained thought life. Someone within the marriage begins to think on things that are not true and eventually embraces the thoughts, and the marriage is devoured over time. A teenager begins entertaining thoughts that should be rejected immediately, and eventually rebels against their parents. Both the divorce and the rebellion began with simple little thoughts.

Whether we like to admit it or not, failure to maintain our thought life is the cause of all the unhealthy activities that men allow into their lives. Ultimately, what gives birth to the embracing of false doctrine is an unmaintained thought life. The person who is controlled by worry, depression, discouragement, lust, and ungodly habits is showing evidence that he has failed to maintain his thought life properly. The person who continues in unforgiveness toward their fellow man has become another casualty of the war within the mind. All these evils are conceived and birthed by entertaining a simple little thought, idea, or suggestion. It is the devil, the deceiver of the world, who presents suggestions to us and then encourages us to embrace thoughts that are not true.

The Works of the Flesh

Paul, writing to the church of Galatia said, *"Now the works of the flesh are manifest, which are these; adultery, fornication, uncleanness, lasciviousness, idolatry, witchcraft, hatred, variance, emulations, wrath, strife, seditions, heresies, envyings, murders, drunkenness, revellings, and such like: of the which I tell you before, as I have also told you in time past, that they which do such things shall not inherit the kingdom of God"* (Gal. 5:19-21).

First of all, notice the phrase "and such like," implying that this is but a short list of what the person who is governed by his flesh will produce. But as important as controlling the flesh is, what is more important is our current thought: every work of the flesh has its beginning within us as we fail to maintain our thought life properly. When a person commits adultery, they are sim-

Losing the battle within the mind will eventually show up in our flesh.

ply revealing that there was a war fought first within their mind and they lost. No one ever commits adultery without thinking about it first. A thought will always precede an action.

When a person is dominated by worry, it reveals plainly that a war raged within their mind and they lost. When a person has lost all hope, they are simply supplying us with the evidence that at some earlier time a war raged within their mind and they lost.

Losing the battle within the mind will eventually show up in our flesh. Losing this battle will eventually affect our relationships with our spouse, parents, relatives, and friends. Losing the battle within the mind can also have a devastating impact on our physical and mental health.

Multitudes of good people are losing this battle within the mind, and God's people seem to be completely unaware of the basic issues at hand. This became apparent to me as I observed a church endeavoring to restore a saint who had committed adultery. As the restoration process began, certain boundaries were put into place. The person being restored was encouraged not to call or see the individual with whom the adulterous act was committed. Weekly sessions were imposed during which the person being restored was required to meet with someone who monitored how much they were reading their Bible and whether or not they had completely read other suggested books. The church attendance of the person being restored was also monitored, along with the amount of time they spent in prayer. As I observed all of these things, I could not help but think, *All of these issues are good. However, if we only monitor surface issues and fail to recognize and monitor the root of the problem, are we really moving this person forward as we should be?*

In order to eradicate and keep adultery out of an individual's life, we must teach them how to maintain their thought life properly. It's not enough to encourage the person to break all ties with the other party, read their Bible, and pray. A person can meet all of these outward requirements and have their thought life remain on the same unbridled path it was on before they were caught. The thought life of a person must be maintained if life changes are to be made. If the thought life is not maintained properly, the ungodly lifestyle will resurface in the future.

Lest you conclude that this book is directed entirely toward those within the Christian community who live ungodly lifestyles, I must tell you this: I am particularly concerned with those who are endeavoring to obtain healing by faith. We must understand the importance of maintaining our thought life. Without this understanding, we will succumb to the onslaught of the devil. As we stand in faith for our healing, we will embrace thoughts that could eventually lead us into failure.

Therefore, I believe it is important for us to learn how to maintain our thought life while we work, in our relationships, or concerning everyday fears. Learning how to maintain our thought life in these areas will serve as a training ground for the greater battle for our physical health. If we fail to maintain our thoughts and attitudes about our spouse or our employer, do we really believe that we can withstand the doubts that will come our way as we endeavor to believe for our healing? I think not.

I believe we must develop the habit of maintaining our thought life concerning the issues of life that are not deadly, so that when we do encounter a life-and-death physical issue, we have already tried and perfected the habit. In many cases, our success or failure depends on how well we respond to the thoughts, ideas, and suggestions that come our way as we stand in faith for our healing.

In the final analysis, what happened to Eve, Jesus, Judas, Ananias, Sapphira, and Lucifer was recorded for our learning. If they could speak today, they would surely admonish us to watch vigilantly over what we think on. We must understand the importance of maintaining our thought life properly.

One Final Question

There is one question that warrants attention before we move on to reveal how we are to use our Bible armour to win the battle within our mind. When Lucifer fell from his lofty position among God's heavenly host, where did his thoughts to dethrone God come from? Great question! And knowing the answer will teach us something valuable about ourselves.

It is evident from our understanding of what happened to Eve, Judas, Ananias, and Sapphira that their thoughts came from the devil himself. But concerning Lucifer while he was in the angelic host serving God, the question comes as to what evil force hurled these thoughts of dethroning God toward him? The answer is a surprising "none"! Then where did these thoughts come from? *They came from what he saw.*

This is more significant than we may first realize. Often we assume all thoughts of lust, pride, and other sins proceed immediately from the devil. They do not. Thoughts will be generated not only by the devil himself, but also by what we see and hear. We must understand that not every thought that enters our mind comes from the devil. Some thoughts enter our life through the eye gate. Other thoughts enter through the ear gate.

The Eye Gate and the Ear Gate

For example, David's desire to have Bathsheba for himself came into his mind as he *observed* her taking a bath. Thoughts about her did not come into his life until he saw her (2 Sam. 11:2-5). The devil is nowhere mentioned in this story, but David certainly suffered drastic consequences for failing to maintain his thought life. He entertained thoughts that he allowed to enter his life through his eye gate.

When the children of Israel *heard* about the giants and the walled cities in the land, thoughts such as "It is impossible to take possession of the Promised Land" suddenly came into their mind. Until they heard from the spies, they believed strongly that the land was theirs for the taking (*see* Numbers chapters 13 and 14). Discouraging thoughts gained entrance into their life through their ear gate, they embraced the thoughts, and they turned their back on the promised land, believing that they could not possess it. They did not obtain the quality of life that God intended for them because they failed to maintain their thought life. Nowhere does the

Bible say that the devil was the one responsible for keeping them out of the Promised Land.

Therefore, it is clear that not every thought comes from the devil himself. But whether thoughts come from the devil, through what we see, or through what we hear, we must be diligent to maintain our thought life. If we are not, those thoughts may very well bring us into the same "land of disappointment" that David and the Israelites walked in.

No wonder Paul said to bring ". . . *into captivity every thought to the obedience of Christ*" (2 Cor. 10:5). "Every thought" means *every* thought, no matter the source.

Whom may the devil devour? He may devour those who have failed to maintain their thought life properly. We are slowly beginning to understand why Paul encouraged us to put on the whole armour of God. Determine this day that you will *not* be one of those whom the devil *may* devour!

Winning the Battle Within the Mind

We have established the fact that our enemy is out to devour us and that he uses thoughts, ideas, and suggestions to accomplish his task. We have also learned that failure to maintain our thought life will eventually lead to our demise.

Furthermore, we discovered that our loving Heavenly Father has not left us unequipped to protect ourselves. We have been given armour—not just one piece, but the *whole* armour of God. Our armour is not made out of metal, but rather knowledge. Our armour is what we know about the truth, righteousness, the gospel of peace, faith, salvation, and the Word of God.

So where do we begin? How do we use our Bible knowledge to maintain our thought life? How do we use what we know in order to defend ourselves against the thoughts that our enemy hurls at us? How do we use the armour of God to maintain our thought life? Here we go . . .

Thought Identification

Knowledge and its proper use wins battles, and the proper use of what we know begins with *thought identification*! The identification of each thought that comes our way must be our first line of defense.

Thought identification requires the examination of every thought in the light of what we know. And this identification process must not be limited only to fear-ridden thoughts or to thoughts that suggest failure or defeat. Keep in mind what we learned from Lucifer's encounters with Eve and Jesus: the devil did not approach them with fear-laden thoughts. The thoughts that the devil used were not filled with anxiety or great dread. But rather, we found that his thoughts came in the same manner and tone as would the advice of a friend who is informing us of privileges previously unknown to us. Remember, the devil is a deceiver. Therefore, we must investigate *every* thought as it approaches to determine if it is friend or foe.

The investigation of every thought must also include thoughts that seem to be using our own voice. For some reason, many have concluded that when the devil approaches us, he will use a different-sounding voice. But every thought that I have ever had—whether it came from God, from what I see or hear, or from the devil—has always sounded exactly like me. I have never had a thought that sounded like someone else's voice. Therefore, every thought must be investigated if we are to maintain our thought life properly.

Investigation begins with questions. Each thought must be scrutinized by asking one question: Does the approaching thought agree with my armour? Does this thought seeking entrance into my life agree with what I know about the truth, my righteousness, my salvation, and faith? Does it agree with what I know about the gospel of peace and the Word of God? Does this thought agree with my Bible-formed beliefs? If the thoughts that are coming my way do not agree with my armour, then at that instant I am to view those thoughts as dangerous, as something to be avoided.

Examine Every Thought

Some might say, "Now wait a minute. Do you mean to tell me that I am to examine *every* thought?" Listen to what Paul says, and notice the words "every thought." Second Corinthians 10:5 says, *"Casting down imaginations, and EVERY high thing that exalteth itself against the knowledge of God, and bringing into captivity EVERY THOUGHT to the obedience of Christ."*

I am reminded of what Peter said in First Peter 5:8,9: *"Be sober, be VIGILANT; because your adversary the devil, as a roaring lion, walketh about, seeking whom he may devour: whom resist stedfast in the faith, knowing that the same afflictions are accomplished in your brethren that are in the world."* The word "vigilant" implies *ever on your guard.*

If we are to win this battle within the mind, we must be *ever on our guard.* This implies constant vigilance, a relentless evaluation of each thought. Some might say that this is a little too much to ask. But wait a minute. We are talking about a war. We are talking about an enemy who is endeavoring to devour us. To attain victory, we must expect to put forth a little extra effort. Failing to do so will mean certain defeat.

Many have experienced the consequences of failing to maintain their thought life. For some, it has cost them their marriage. For others, it has cost them the price of no longer being able to enjoy a healthy, balanced relationship with their children. For still others, it has cost them their job, peace of mind, or health. Some have become addicted to pornography. Many are slaves to depression or hatred. The list of casualties goes on and on. In my opinion, the price is too high. I would rather pay the small price of complying with God's instructions than experience the huge price of failing to do so. The consequences are too great!

In Ephesians 6:10-17 and 2 Corinthians 10:3-5, Paul chose the symbolism of war to stress the importance of maintaining our mind. I will follow suit. During wartime, camp is set up—a perimeter is established. Once the perimeter is established, guards are posted at various points. Their responsibility is to stand guard and protect the perimeter. The degree of their vigilance determines the degree of safety that those inside the camp will enjoy. When the guards are on duty, each person seeking entrance into the camp is stopped and searched. Their vehicle is thoroughly inspected for items such as guns, bombs, or drugs. Is it work? Yes! But the extra effort is a must! The safety of the camp is at stake. Heightened security is the price that must be paid if the enemy is to be kept out of the camp.

So it is with our minds. This is a war that each one of us is in, whether we like it or not. Our enemy is walking about seeking whom he may devour. If we are to keep him from infiltrating our life, we must investigate each thought that comes our way. The greater our need for victory, the greater the necessity for us to examine every thought.

Each Thought Has Life or Death Attached to It

Every thought, every idea, every suggestion—no matter how innocent, how simple, or how casual it appears—must be investigated. Why is this? Because every thought has a life or death component attached to it! We have never had a thought come our way that did not have some type of life attached to it. A thought either has a death nature attached to it or it has a "zoe life" nature attached to it. *Zoe* is a Greek word meaning "the God-kind of life" or "life as God has it."

Once a thought is allowed access into our life, the nature or life within that thought is released within our life and begins its work. For example, here is an innocent thought that we all have had: *"Snub them. Give them the cold shoulder."* Attached to this simple thought is a relationship-destroying nature or component. This simple suggestion has within it the ability to destroy a relationship that may have taken years to develop. The moment this idea is embraced and acted upon, our relationship with the individual begins to deteriorate. Are we beginning to comprehend the importance of investigating every thought?

It's kind of like the little thought that might come to you in a store: *"Just put the packet of gum into your pocket. No one will ever know. They will never miss it."* This may be a little suggestion; but are we aware that there is jail time attached to that thought? If that thought is not scrutinized—if we fail to examine it up against what we know from the Word—it can cost us much more than the twenty-five cents that was required by the store in the first place.

The thought might come to you on your job, *"The boss does not appreciate you. Your ideas are not even considered. Slack up, slow down, take it easy. They don't care about you anyway."* If you entertain those ideas long enough, you will find yourself embracing them as truth. But do we understand that the poison contained within this little thought has the potential to lead us not only into ungodly behavior on the job but also eventually into financial disaster?

Every thought has some type of negative or positive nature attached to it, no matter how innocent that thought seems. For example, perhaps you have just exerted a tremendous amount of effort to get to church on time because your pastor will be speaking today. The song service begins and there is no sign of him. Then the offering is received, and still there is no sign of your pastor. After the special music, the associate pastor stands up and announces that the pastor is snowed in at O'Hare Airport in Chicago and therefore he, the associate pastor, will be speaking today. And the moment you hear those words, the thought hits you: *"Great. I never get anything listening to him. What a waste of effort. I could still be in bed cozy and snug. But nooooo!"* Just a simple little thought. But it has a "not-going-to-get-anything-out-of-this-service" nature attached to it. If you embrace the thought, then the nature attached to the thought is released within your life and, sure enough, you go away with nothing from his message.

Failing to thoroughly investigate every thought is as dangerous as failing to thoroughly investigate every car and driver approaching the entrance to the camp during a war. Slothfulness could cost us dearly.

Remember the thoughts that Ananias and Sapphira encountered? *"Just keep back part of the price, but tell everyone that you have given it all to the church. The leaders of the church will think much more highly of you if you do."* Ananias and Sapphira embraced the idea, but they did not comprehend that this little idea had a death nature attached to it. We must evaluate every thought in the light of what we have been taught from the Bible if we are to obtain and maintain victory.

This investigation process is an action that we must carry out continually in every area of our life. We must not go by how dangerous a thought looks in order to determine our degree of response. The level of our response to every thought should be exactly the same, whether we are dealing with a slothful-work thought or a "you're-not-going-to-be-healed-this-time" thought.

Always Be Ready

We must always be ready to investigate every thought, whether it comes at a convenient time or not, to determine whether it agrees with our Bible knowledge. This may mean that we examine the thoughts about not getting healed this time up against the Word while we lay in bed awake at three o'clock in the morning. Dear reader, our enemy, the devil, does not care if you are wide-awake or half-awake. If he can accomplish his mission of persuading you to embrace one of his thoughts as truth and act upon it, he wins. It's impossible to stop thoughts from coming our way, but it *is* possible to avoid embracing the thoughts that are from the wicked one if we will just spend a short time investigating each incoming thought.

Vigilance Is Required

When we desire freedom from a habit, vigilance must be the force that motivates us to examine every suggestion that touches the arena we seek victory in. We must scrutinize even the slightest, most innocent thought in the light of our Bible knowledge to determine whether it is a friend or a foe. Whether it comes through the mind, ears, or eyes, each thought must be investigated to determine whether or not it agrees with what we know or, in other words, our armour. I am talking about *thought identification.*

Limited Bible Knowledge Handicaps Us

The disadvantaged Christian is the one who has limited knowledge or no knowledge. These dear saints will be found accepting most every thought that comes their way. They are easy prey because they have no point of reference to determine whether the thought is true or not.

Most of us were in this position when we first considered the possibility of becoming born again. As we considered accepting the Lord into our life, the thought came: *"You're not good enough. Furthermore, your past has too much sin in it. God loving you? Impossible!"* Those who lacked Bible knowledge found it easy to accept this thought as true and walked away without responding to the outstretched arms of our loving Savior. On the other hand, those who knew God's love for people who have sin in their life could defeat those thoughts and respond completely to our Savior's call. Compliance was made possible by a thorough investigation of the "too-much-sin-in-your-life" thought. The thought was found to be misleading and exalting itself against the knowledge of God. It was found to disagree with our Bible-formed beliefs.

Until Jesus Returns or 'Till Death Do Us Part'

I wish I could tell you that when you turn sixty-five years of age, you will no longer need to investigate each thought that comes your way. But that would be misleading. Our enemy will be our enemy until either Jesus returns or "till death do us part." Therefore, we must develop the habit of investigating each and every thought.

We must also get past the mentality that we only need to investigate every thought while we are endeavoring to obtain victory in a specific area. We cannot give in to the idea that once we are enjoying the good life with health, peace, and prosperity, then we can lighten up a bit on this "every thought" business. This kind of thinking will get us into major trouble. Our enemy is walking about as a roaring lion seeking whom he may devour, and he is considering not only the down-and-outers but also the rich and the famous. No matter our status in life, we must all be about the business of investigating every thought if we are to reach or maintain the level of life that our Heavenly Father has for us.

Important Instructions—Read Carefully

As thoughts come to you, I encourage you to begin forming the habit of examining them by asking yourself, Does this thought agree with my armour? Does it agree with what I have been taught from God's Word? Does it agree with what I know about the truth, faith, righteousness, the Word of God, the gospel of peace, or my salvation? These questions must stand between us

Thoughts can be diagnosed within seconds of their appearance.

and each thought that comes our way. This process does not require hours of our time, but rather seconds. Thoughts can be diagnosed within seconds of their appearance.

In essence, if we have not discovered a thought recently that goes against our Bible armour, it may be a good indication that we are not doing a very good job of investigating every thought. If we have not said *no* to a thought in a while, this also could indicate that we are not doing that great a job of maintaining our thought life.

I encourage you to stop for a moment and reflect. Ask yourself these questions: How aware am I of this principle? Do I measure the thoughts I have against what I know from the Bible? Or do I go about my daily chores with absolutely no consciousness of my responsibility in this arena? Your answers to these simple questions will reveal how well you are investigating every thought that comes your way.

Our Final Duty

As we previously stated, the maintenance of our thought life begins as we investigate each thought by determining whether or not it agrees with our armour of Bible knowledge. The objective is to identify which thoughts should be allowed access into our life and which thoughts should be kept out. Therefore, each thought is to pass through the filtering system of what we know about the truth, righteousness, the gospel of peace, faith, salvation, and the Word of God. Each thought is to be interrogated by asking it, "Do you agree with what I believe that has been formed within me from God's Word? Do you agree with the armour that God has provided for me within His Word?"

Identify, Quench, and Capture

Once we discover a thought that disagrees with what we believe, the battle begins. There is no battle when the enemy hurls one of his thoughts at us and we openly embrace it. No, the battle begins when we identify the thought as coming from the deceiver. But the battle is won as we quench the thought and bring it into captivity.

Paul instructed us "to quench all the fiery darts of the wicked" (Eph. 6:16) and "to cast down imaginations, and every high thing that exalts itself against the knowledge of God, and bring into captivity every thought to the obedience of Christ" (2 Cor. 10:5).

Quench

Identifying a thought as a foe is the first step toward the maintenance of our mind. The second step is that of quenching the approaching thought. Therefore, we must understand what it means to quench. The word "quench" is very interesting. It means *to extinguish*. A fire is extinguished as we cut off or remove its fuel source. *The fuel source of thoughts is attention.* When we remove the attention factor from the thought, we are in essence quenching the thought.

The life span of a thought is determined by the amount of attention it receives.

The life span of a thought is determined by the amount of attention it receives. And the strength of a thought either increases or decreases depending on how much attention that thought is given.

Entertaining the possibilities—mulling them over in your mind—is exactly what a thought requires in order to thrive. The more you entertain thoughts, the more they grow in strength. It's like adding another car to a freight train. The more cars you add, the harder it becomes to stop the train.

On the other hand, turning your attention away from a thought and on to other things is a thought's worst enemy. When you are confronted with an attacking thought, turning your attention to what the Bible says has the same effect on that thought as turning your back on someone who is speaking to you and beginning a conversation with another person. Doing that to me would make me angry. And that's my very point: thoughts detest being ignored. They flourish when they have your complete attention.

Therefore, the act of quenching begins as we redirect our attention away from the attacking thought and on to what we believe about the truth, righteousness, the gospel of peace, faith, salvation, and the Word of God. Once your attention has been redirected from the thought to the Word, your battle is half won! Glory!

A Decision of Your Will

The redirection of our attention will be the result of a decision of our will. This is not something that happens within us automatically. It occurs only within the vigilant. It occurs only within those who are making a conscious effort to maintain their thought life.

For example, let's say you're working on your job and suddenly the thought hits you, "*Slow down. Your boss is not even here today. Take it easy.*" Then another thought speaks up and says, "*You know, you do more than your share of work around here. If anyone deserves a slow night, it's you. You deserve a break today!*"

But because you have been working on developing the habit of maintaining your thought life, you quickly put the thought to the test. You investigate it by examining it up against your Bible armour, and you find it wanting. You find that this little "*slow-down— you-deserve-a-break-today*" thought goes completely against what the Bible teaches. And you think to yourself, *The enemy has just hurled a fiery dart at me.* Congratulations! You have just used your armour to identify a thought that originated from the enemy.

Understanding the severity of this conflict, you immediately initiate the quenching process. You begin by redirecting your attention to what the Bible says. You begin to remind yourself of all the scriptures that speak of how you are to conduct yourself on your job as a Christian—scriptures such as:

He becometh poor that dealeth with a slack hand: but the hand of the diligent maketh rich.

—Proverbs 10:4

Seest thou a man diligent in his business? he shall stand before kings; he shall not stand before mean men.

—Proverbs 22:29

Slothfulness casteth into a deep sleep; and an idle soul shall suffer hunger.

—Proverbs 19:15

For even when we were with you, this we commanded you, that if any would not work, neither should he eat.

—2 Thessalonians 3:10

Servants, obey in all things your masters according to the flesh; not with eyeservice, as menpleasers; but in singleness of heart, fearing God: And whatsoever ye do, do it heartily, as to the Lord, and not unto men; Knowing that of the Lord ye shall receive the reward of the inheritance: for ye serve the Lord Christ. But he that doeth wrong shall receive for the wrong which he hath done: and there is no respect of persons.

—Colossians 3:22-25

Exhort servants to be obedient unto their own masters, and to please them well in all things; not answering again; Not purloining, but shewing all good fidelity; that they may adorn the doctrine of God our Saviour in all things.

—Titus 2:9,10

The entire time you are thinking about what the Bible says, you are, in effect, extinguishing the attacking thought. The *"slow-down—you-deserve-a-break-to-day"* thought is slowly being depleted of its strength by the lack of attention. Your mind has been redirected; it is busy thinking on whatsoever things are true, honest, just, pure, lovely, and of a good report (Phil. 4:8). You suddenly begin to realize that you are on the path that is leading you to victory! You are being a doer of the Word and not just a hearer! You are quenching fiery darts! Congratulations!

Capture

Good for you. You have identified the approaching thought as being a foe. You have turned your attention off of the thought and onto the Word of God. And now, the third and final step toward victory in this battle is to bring this "foe of a thought" into captivity. Second Corinthians 10:5 says, *"Casting down imaginations, and every high thing that exalteth itself against the knowledge of God, and bringing into captivity every thought to the obedience of Christ."*

Paul admonishes us to bring into captivity *every* thought. Look carefully at the following phrase and consider it prayerfully: *Learn how thoughts take you captive and you can learn how to take thoughts captive.*

Consider for a moment the word "capture." When a thought is out to capture us, it brings with it "friends."

In other words, a thought cannot capture us without assistance any more than one person can capture me by himself. If you desire to capture me, you will have to bring some friends with you. In order to capture me, you will have to surround me.

As a thought approaches us in order to capture us, it brings friends with it. These so-called friends will provide further evidence to verify the truthfulness of the attacking thought. I have had thoughts bring with them videotape, audiotape, and even still photos. Each piece of evidence provides proof that the suggestion is true. Each reminds us of events in the past that prove the attacking thought is true. Their ultimate goal is to persuade us to embrace the thought, to accept the thought as truth. The more evidence the attacking thought can present that points to its truthfulness, the easier it becomes for the thought to capture us. *Learn how thoughts take you captive and you can learn how to take thoughts captive.*

How Thoughts Turn Relationships Sour

For example, suddenly the thought hits you, *"So-and-so does not like you."* The instant that thought comes, your mind is flooded with pieces of evidence that suggest that this thought is true. The first piece of evidence is turned on, and through a mental videotape player you see yourself walking the main corridor of your local shopping mall. Suddenly you see So-and-so heading toward you, and when your eyes meet, So-and-so immediately turns and goes into the nearest store. The videotape is turned off and a little voice says, *"See, So-and-so does not like you. You know they saw you, but when you both made eye contact they immediately turned and walked into Sears."*

Then the audiotape is turned on and you recognize what you hear as being the last phone conversation that you had with So-and-so. As the tape plays, the thought comes to you, *"Listen to the tone of their voice. There is no sincerity in it at all. In fact, it almost sounds like they have their mind on other things while they are talking to you. And remember how quickly they endeavored to end the conversation?"* The audiotape is turned off and a little voice says once again, *"You know it's true. So-and-so does not like you."* Of course, all of this happens at split-second speed.

Next, this thought that has you almost surrounded brings out the still photos. The 5x7 photo is a picture of you at Christmastime opening gifts, and suddenly you realize that you did not get a gift from So-and-so. And the thought hits your mind again, *"See, So-and-so does not like you."* And before you know it, you find yourself agreeing with the thought and your feelings toward that individual begin to turn sour.

Dear reader, do you understand that if you were that person in this little scenario, then you just became a casualty of the war that Paul spoke to us about in Ephesians?

And it all came about because you embraced the thoughts without any input from your armour. Therefore, you soon found yourself thinking about that person in a very negative way. And before you knew it, your words about them changed, your actions toward them changed, and your relationship with So-and-so began to deteriorate. And it all began because you failed to investigate a simple little thought, idea, or suggestion that came your way. You failed to stand against a wile of the devil.

Relationships are allowed to dissolve, not because some evil power forces us to act differently toward the other person, but rather because little thoughts enter into our mind unrestricted and are allowed to grow within us. It's the little foxes that spoil the vines (*see* Song of Sol. 2:15).

Depression

This process is exactly how we enter into depression. A little suggestion comes your way, insinuating that *"things are only going to get worse in your marriage."* And before you know it, every uncaring deed that your husband has ever committed suddenly flashes before your eyes. Every episode that displayed a lack of respect and selfishness is as fresh as the day it happened. After a time of dwelling on all the evidence, this wife slowly slips into full-blown depression and another day is ruined. It is ruined because she failed to maintain her thought life properly. She did not take the time to filter the incoming thoughts through her armour. Her depression began with a little thought, idea, or suggestion that brought enough friends with it to capture her.

Employees

Employees slip into a state of hopelessness on their jobs in much the same way. When the employee loses hope, slothfulness will be his constant companion. This hopelessness can be birthed within an employee through a simple thought such as, *"You're out of the loop. Your days are numbered. They don't care about you and your ideas any more."*

If that single thought comes alone, we will not give it "the time of day." If it comes with not one piece of evidence, our enemy knows that we will not entertain it. But when it can produce other pieces of evidence that support its case, the war to capture us has begun.

Healing

Have you ever noticed how the thoughts come as you endeavor to believe God for physical healing? Fiery darts that are filled with doubt and unbelief come, such as, *"If you really believed, don't you think that you would be healed by now? Have you ever heard of anyone being healed of what you have? Remember sister So-and-so? She had the exact same thing and she died, and you're not half as spiritual as she was!"*

Before you know it, your hope of being healed has been replaced by doubts and deep feelings of hopelessness. All this is the result of a little thought that was successful in its endeavors to capture you.

If only we would become aware of our responsibility to allow our armour to confront and investigate each thought! Oh, how quickly we would be able to identify these thoughts as evil things that are out to limit our ability to receive God's best. I am sure that we would have put up a much greater fight if only we had recognized the incoming thoughts as fiery darts.

Learn How Thoughts Capture You
You Can Learn How to Capture Thoughts

It is clear: in order for a thought to capture us, it must bring with it other thoughts that support its case. Working together, they endeavor to overwhelm us with evidence. When the "friends" of the thought speak up, they present evidence that appears to support the validity of the attacking thought. They remind us of events and statements made by others that provide evidence that the attacking thought is legitimate.

Since we understand how thoughts capture us, we now have an advantage. Therefore, once a thought has been identified as a foe, we then must quench it. We do that by turning our attention off of the thought and onto what the Word of God has to say about the suggestion or idea that the approaching thought is offering. Lastly, we must turn once again toward the approaching thought. Only this time we are accompanied by *our* friends—passages and scriptures from God's Word that provide proof that the approaching thought is false. As we turn toward the thought, we begin to allow what we have found in God's Word to flow out of our mouth.

Yes, dear friend, if thoughts speak to us, then we must speak to them. We must use our mouth and begin to quote what the Bible says. We must begin to quote what our armour says. Let *your* "friends" present their evidence!

Use Your Voice

The more scriptures you gather, the more "friends" you are assembling. You are gathering evidence that you will use to capture the thought—to surround the attacking thought. As you mull over the Bible passages, begin to allow them to speak. Using your voice, let each passage present its case verbally. With your mouth, speak your evidence. If thoughts speak to us in order to capture us, then we must speak to them in order to capture them. Follow their example and imitate them in this respect. Speak! We capture thoughts by speaking to them!

> *If thoughts speak to us in order to capture us, then we must speak to them in order to capture them.*

Speak to the attacking thought exactly as our Lord Jesus illustrated for us in Luke chapter 4:

"It is written . . . ;" "It is written . . . ;" "It is said . . ."
(Luke 4:4,8,12). Let your voice be heard.

The person who refuses to speak—the silent
Christian—will find it difficult to win this battle within
the mind. Therefore, speak with authority and surety,
knowing that in doing so you are defending yourself
against the wiles of the devil. You must not hesitate.
Remember—this is war.

Do you recall the *"slow-down—you-deserve-a-break-
today"* thought? Once your armour has identified the
incoming thought as a fiery dart, then get in the Word
and locate scriptures that support your findings that
the attacking thought goes against your armour. Then,
turn your attention back toward the attacking thought
and begin to speak. Allow your "friends," the scriptures,
to present their case. Your words should sound something like this: "I have determined to be a diligent person, for the hand of the diligent maketh me rich. The
Bible says the diligent will stand before important people but the idle soul shall suffer. I like to eat. Therefore,
I refuse to slow down. I will work diligently. I am to
obey my employer in all things. I am to work heartily as
unto the Lord, for I am determined to adorn the doctrine of God by my behavior on my job."

Speaking your beliefs—speaking what the Word
says—will capture the attacking thought. As you
speak, you are completely surrounding the thought
and, in essence, you are capturing it. And should the

"slow-down—you-deserve-a-break-today" thought come again later on in the day or next week, then repeat the process. Turn your attention back to the Word, gather more evidence that proves that thought is incorrect, and then turn your attention once again toward the thought and start speaking the Bible knowledge you have accumulated. We can win this battle within the mind!

Consequences of the Suggested Action

But what happens if the thought refuses to quit? All of us have had thoughts that return over and over again. May I suggest this further action? When this occurs, go back into the Bible and find scriptures that describe the consequences of the suggested act. Ask yourself this question: What will be produced if I embrace and comply with this thought? For example, if I accept this thought of *"slow down—you deserve a break today,"* what will be the result? Reminding ourselves of the consequences of the suggested act will strengthen us in our resistance.

For example, if I slow down on the job, Proverbs 6:6-11 tells me what will be the outcome.

PROVERBS 6:6-11

6　**Go to the ant, thou sluggard; consider her ways, and be wise:**

7　**Which having no guide, overseer, or ruler,**

8　**Provideth her meat in the summer, and gathereth her food in the harvest.**

9   How long wilt thou sleep, O sluggard? when
    wilt thou arise out of thy sleep?

10 Yet a little sleep, a little slumber, a little fold-
    ing of the hands to sleep:

11 So shall thy poverty come as one that travel-
    leth, and thy want as an armed man.

Once reminded of such things, we again turn toward
the attacking thought and boldly say with our mouth,
"Oh no you don't! I do not need poverty coming to me as
one that travelleth and my want as an armed man. In
addition to that, Proverbs 10:4,5 says, *'He becometh poor
that dealeth with a slack hand: but the hand of the diligent maketh rich. He that gathereth in summer is a wise
son: but he that sleepeth in harvest is a son that causeth
shame.'* No way do I want to invite poverty into my life
just because I worked with a slack hand, just because I
slowed down on the job! Furthermore, if I slow down on
the job as a Christian, it will invite unbelievers to blas-
pheme, or speak evil of, the Name of God and His doctrine, and I do not like that consequence. I will honor
my boss and work to the best of my ability, because the
Bible says, *'Let as many servants as are under the yoke
count their own masters worthy of all honour, that the
name of God and his doctrine be not blasphemed'*
(1 Tim. 6:1)." As we consider the consequences of the
suggested act, it will become clear that, should we comply, the price would be too great. This realization will add
strength to our resolve to properly use our entire armour
of Bible knowledge to stand against the fiery dart.

Speaking with our mouth and presenting our case—using the same technique that attacking thoughts use on us—will enable us to win this battle within our mind. In the end, we must be found properly using what we know. We must use the whole armour of God to identify the approaching thought and to provide us with sufficient proof that we are not alone. Then, accompanied by our "armour"—scriptures that support our position—we can turn our attention toward the thought. Lastly, we must begin to speak with our mouth and allow our "armour," the scriptures, to present their case. As we do, we will be properly using what we know.

In a previous chapter of this book, I offered this principle for your consideration: *Knowledge and its proper use wins battles*. We properly use what we know when we allow our Bible knowledge to identify thoughts as foes and to supply us with evidence, and when we speak out the evidence we have found. Doing that enables us to win the battles within our mind.

Consider Eve, Judas, Ananias, and Sapphira. If only they had properly used what they knew! Oh, how different their stories would have been! But as we consider our precious Jesus, it is evident that He illustrates for us how simple it is to identify, quench, and capture the fiery darts of the wicked one. The truth is plain: *Knowledge and its proper use does win battles!*

Finally, My Brethren . . .

Now you can understand why I feel so strongly that maintaining our thought life is a key to addressing the issues presented at the beginning of this book. Failure to do so will allow all of the pollutants of humanity into our life. Worry, depression, frustration, suicide, tempers, hatred, lying, stealing, adultery, fornication, hopelessness, envy, pride, selfishness, divorce, rebellion, false doctrine, and the like will continue to reign within our lives as long as we are unaware of our responsibility to bridle or maintain our thought life. For all of these things begin with nothing more than a simple thought, idea, or suggestion.

Our marriages will continue to be weakened and our performance on our jobs will remain below God's standards as long as Christians continue to allow any and all thoughts to enter their minds at will. Our inability to receive healing through faith will continue to frustrate us as long as we fail to examine every thought that comes our way after we pray and believe that we receive.

Since the 1960s

I find it very interesting that since the 1960s, our generation has been taught much concerning the importance of our words. We have been instructed and encouraged to put a watch over our mouth.

We have also been instructed to bridle our conduct—our behavior—or, in other words, what we do. We have been taught to "keep our body under," to "bring it into subjection." We have been informed that if we choose to allow our body to do whatever it wishes, doing so will allow consequences into our life that will ultimately dishonor God.

While it is true that we must guard what we say and bridle our conduct in order to keep the devil from infiltrating our life, it seems to me that we have left open the main door that he uses to gain entrance into our life. We have left open the door of our mind. It's almost as if we are standing guard over Door Number One, and we are protecting Door Number Two, but the enemy is gaining entrance into our life through Door Number Three—the very door that we have almost completely ignored! Door Number Three appears to be the door of our mind.

I believe one reason this subject has not been addressed as it should be is that it is a little easier for the church to chart a person's progress concerning how well he is guarding what he says. It is a little easier to monitor how well a person is bridling his conduct than how well he is controlling his thoughts. Whether we like it or not, the only ones who really know how well we are maintaining our thought life are God and us individually. This places the complete responsibility for the maintenance of our thoughts upon us. The mission, if we choose to accept it, is ours alone.

But be sure of this one thing, dear reader: What you allow into your mind and think on long enough will eventually manifest itself either through your words or through your actions. There is an old saying that comes to mind that goes something like this: "Be sure your sins will find you out." We may not be able to monitor each other's daily progress. But the time will come when, through our words or through our actions, everyone will be able to determine just how well we have done in this arena of the maintenance of our minds.

Putting on the whole armour of God gives us the ability to identify, quench, and capture the thoughts, ideas, and suggestions that endeavor to exalt themselves against the knowledge of God.

Knowledge and its proper use wins battles!

A Word of Encouragement

No wonder Paul encouraged us so strongly to put on the *whole armour* of God. For it will take using all of what we know from the Bible to win this conflict within our mind. It is comforting to know that our God has supplied us with numerous scriptures that enable us to detect and defeat any and all thoughts that our enemy may hurl at us. There is not a thought that our enemy can hurl at us that our God has not equipped us with scriptures to detect and defeat. Our responsibility is to find the appropriate scriptures and use them properly.

In the end, it will take *consistent effort* on our part if we choose to defend ourselves against the fiery darts of the wicked one. It will take *effort to investigate* each thought in order to determine whether it is a friend or a foe. It will take *effort to locate scriptures* that we can use to surround and ultimately capture the incoming thought. And lastly, it will take *effort to speak what we*

know toward the incoming thought that is seeking to
spread its fire of destruction within our life.

This is true no matter the issue, no matter the
thought. The attack could be thoughts that seek to
spread doubt concerning your chances of receiving healing through faith. Or, it could be thoughts that are
encouraging ungodly behavior. It might be thoughts that
suggest how unworthy you are or that your spouse will
never love you like they did before. When these thoughts
come, I encourage you to turn to the Word of God. Locate
scriptures that address the specific area in which you
are being attacked. If you are having difficulty finding
passages within the Bible that address your battle, I
encourage you to obtain a reference book from your local
Christian bookstore called *Nave's Topical Bible*. This
Bible aid lists topics along with scriptural references for
each. It is an excellent tool for finding passages that
address the issues that we encounter daily.

Should this resource fail to address the area in
which you are currently facing an attack, I encourage
you to contact your pastor or church. Inform them of the
area that you are having difficulty with and ask them to
suggest scriptures that you may use in order to defend
yourself mentally.

We are in a war, and the price for failing to maintain
our thought life is great. Make the decision now to begin
to take what you know and use it properly. Maintain
your thought life, whether toward your spouse, children,

parents, friends, job, finances, health, or your Heavenly Father and how you see yourself in relationship to Him. Endeavor to bridle your thoughts with the Word of God. If for some reason you find yourself slipping, run to First John 1:9 and ask the Father to forgive you. Then return to the task of vigilantly guarding what you allow your mind to dwell on. For knowledge and its proper use wins battles!

May God's grace and power be with you as you take unto yourself the whole armour of God!

Enjoy these other great books by Doug Jones!

Positioning Yourself to Receive Healing

By DOUG JONES

Where are you on your quest to receive healing? In this book, Rev. Jones presents key beliefs that one must embrace and act upon in order to be properly positioned to receive healing.

$10.95 ISBN-13: 978-0-89276-965-0

Understanding the Healing Power of God

By DOUG JONES

This book presents with simple yet profound clarity the truth concerning this seldom-discussed subject: understanding God's healing power. When we connect our faith to God's power, we are on the path to victory!

$10.95 ISBN-13: 978-0-89276-964-3

To order, visit rhema.org/store or call 1-888-258-0999.

"What should I do with my life?"

If you've been asking yourself this question, **RHEMA BIBLE TRAINING COLLEGE is a good place to come and find out.** RBTC will build a solid biblical foundation in you that will carry you through—wherever life takes you.

The Benefits:

◆ Training at *the* **top Spirit-filled Bible school**

◆ Teaching based on steadfast faith in God's Word

◆ Unique two-year core program specially designed to **grow** you as a believer, help you **recognize the voice of God**, and equip you to **live successfully**

◆ Optional **specialized training** in the third- and fourth-year program of your choice: Biblical Studies, Helps Ministry, Itinerant Ministry, Pastoral Ministry, Student Ministries, Worship, World Missions, and General Extended Studies

◆ **Accredited** with Transworld Accrediting Commission International

◆ Worldwide **ministry opportunities**— while you're in school

Apply today!
1-888-28-FAITH (1-888-283-2484)
rbtc.org

Rhema Word Partner Club

WORKING *together* TO REACH THE WORLD!

People. Power. Purpose.

Have you ever dropped a stone into water? Small waves rise up at the point of impact and travel in all directions. It's called a ripple effect. That's the kind of impact Christians are meant to have in this world—the kind of impact that the Rhema family is producing in the earth today.

The Rhema Word Partner Club links Christians with a shared interest in reaching people with the Gospel and the message of faith in God.

Together we are reaching across generations, cultures, and nations to spread the Good News of Jesus Christ to every corner of the earth.

To join us in reaching the world,
visit **rhema.org/wpc** or call **1-866-312-0972**.

Always on.

For the latest news and information on products, media, podcasts, study resources, and special offers, visit us online 24 hours a day.

rhema.org

Free Subscription!

Call now to receive a free subscription to *The Word of Faith* magazine from Kenneth Hagin Ministries. Receive encouragement and spiritual refreshment from . . .

- *Faith-building articles from Kenneth W. Hagin, Lynette Hagin, Craig W. Hagin, and others*

- *"Timeless Teaching" from the archives of Kenneth E. Hagin*

- *Feature articles on prayer and healing*

- *Testimonies of salvation, healing, and deliverance*

- *Children's activity page*

- *Updates on Rhema Bible Training College, Rhema Bible Church, and other outreaches of Kenneth Hagin Ministries*

Subscribe today for your free *Word of Faith*!

1-888-28-FAITH (1-888-283-2484)

rhema.org/wof

Rhema
Correspondence Bible School

The Rhema Correspondence Bible School is a home Bible study course that can help you in your everyday life!

This course of study has been designed with you in mind, providing practical teaching on prayer, faith, healing, Spirit-led living, and much more to help you live a victorious Christian life!

Flexible

Enroll any time: choose your topic of study;
study at your own pace!

Affordable

Pay as you go—only $35 per lesson!
(Price subject to change without notice.)

Profitable

"The Lord has blessed me through a Rhema Correspondence Bible School graduate. . . . He witnessed to me 15 years ago, and the Lord delivered me from drugs and alcohol. I was living on the streets and then in somebody's tool shed. Now I lead a victorious and blessed life! I now am a graduate of Rhema Correspondence Bible School too! I own a beautiful home. I have a beautiful wife and two children who also love the Lord. The Lord allows me to preach whenever my pastor is out of town. I am on the board of directors at my church and at the Christian school. Thank you, and God bless you and your ministry!"

—D.J., Lusby, Maryland

"Thank you for continually offering Rhema Correspondence Bible School. The eyes of my understanding have been enlightened greatly through the Word of God through having been enrolled in RCBS. My life has forever been changed."

—M.R., Princeton, N.C.

For enrollment information and a course listing, call today!

1-888-28-FAITH (1-888-283-2484)

rhema.org/rcbs

OFFER CODE—BKORD:BRCSC